Messages
from a
Wonderful
Afterlife

To Write to the Author

If you wish to contact the author or would like more information about this book, please write to the author in care of Llewellyn Worldwide Ltd. and we will forward your request. Both the author and publisher appreciate hearing from you and learning of your enjoyment of this book and how it has helped you. Llewellyn Worldwide Ltd. cannot guarantee that every letter written to the author can be answered, but all will be forwarded. Please write to:

Kristy Robinett
℅ Llewellyn Worldwide
2143 Wooddale Drive
Woodbury, MN 55125-2989

Please enclose a self-addressed stamped envelope for reply,
or $1.00 to cover costs. If outside the USA, enclose
an international postal reply coupon.

Many of Llewellyn's authors have websites with additional
information and resources. For more information,
please visit our website at http://www.llewellyn.com

Messages

from a

Wonderful

Afterlife

Signs
Loved Ones
Send from Beyond

KRISTY ROBINETT

Llewellyn Publications
Woodbury, Minnesota

FIRST EDITION
First Printing, 2017

Cover design: Ellen Lawson
Interior art: Llewellyn Art Department

Llewellyn Publications is a registered trademark of Llewellyn Worldwide Ltd.

Library of Congress Cataloging-in-Publication Data
 Names: Robinett, Kristy, author.
  Title: Messages from a wonderful afterlife : signs loved ones send from
   beyond / Kristy Robinett.
  Description: First Edition. | Woodbury : Llewellyn Worldwide, Ltd, 2017. |
   Includes bibliographical references.
  Identifiers: LCCN 2017026784 (print) | LCCN 2017016325 (ebook) | ISBN
   9780738752242 (ebook) | ISBN 9780738750910 (alk. paper)
  Subjects: LCSH: Future life. | Spiritualism.
  Classification: LCC BF1311.F8 (print) | LCC BF1311.F8 R633 2017 (ebook) | .
   DDC
   133.9--dc23
  LC record available at https://lccn.loc.gov/2017026784

Llewellyn Worldwide Ltd. does not participate in, endorse, or have any authority or responsibility concerning private business transactions between our authors and the public.
 All mail addressed to the author is forwarded but the publisher cannot, unless specifically instructed by the author, give out an address or phone number.
 Any Internet references contained in this work are current at publication time, but the publisher cannot guarantee that a specific location will continue to be maintained. Please refer to the publisher's website for links to authors' websites and other sources.

Llewellyn Publications
A Division of Llewellyn Worldwide Ltd.
2143 Wooddale Drive
Woodbury, MN 55125-2989
www.llewellyn.com

Printed in the United States of America

Other Books by Kristy Robinett

Forevermore

It's a Wonderful Afterlife

Messenger Between Worlds

Forthcoming Books by Kristy Robinett

Tails from the Afterlife

Dedication

To the other man I called Dad. May his golf course always be green and lush and his stroke straight.

Contents

Acknowledgments

This book could not have happened without the hundreds of thousands of clients and their loved ones on the Other Side who have touched my life more than I could ever eloquently communicate. I'm so grateful for being a messenger and making the connections.

I'm so grateful to my family, especially my husband Chuck Robinett and all of his love, support, and mad driving skills. To my kids, Micaela Even Kempf and Connor Even, who have always understood my crazy job and the schedule that comes with it, for the hugs when I'm feeling stressed. For the love from my stepdaughters Cora and Molly. And to my dad, who keeps me on my toes, and my mother-in-law, Mary Lou, who has taught us to say it like it is without apology.

Love to my brother, Duane Schiller, and sister, Cheri Ford, for dad-sitting when I have to go out of town.

I am thankful for having some of the best friends ever, especially Mikey and Marjanna McClain, our travel buddies, who so lovingly help us with events and late night laughs.

Mary Byberg, my assistant and friend who's so patient with my clients and with me.

My best friends and confidantes; Gayle Buchan, Donna Shorkey, Laura Bohlman, and Jenni Licata. Thank you to Colleen Kwiecinski and her mad Cooper-sitting skills. Jan, Tomes, Kathy Curatolo, and Ryan Sparks for their friendship and assistance with events. Thank you to Lori Weiss for her insight and support.

Thank you to Dr. David Schindler and Nancy for beautiful care and constant support.

Katie Eaves, thank you for always getting me and trusting me with your crazy entourage of ghosts.

Thank you to Courtney Sierra and her gift of always making my hair look superb, for being the best and most affordable counselor a girl could ever have.

My gratitude goes out to Llewellyn Publishing, especially Amy Glaser, who inspires me daily to reach for my dreams.

I am thankful to my own Spirit Guides for teaching me that learning and exploring never gets old, and that it doesn't necessarily have to take place in a classroom.

And finally, to my mom in Heaven, who reminds me that our loved ones on the Other Side are around us even when we don't feel them beside us and that angels surround us during our happy times and during the darkest times.

Disclaimer

Although the stories are based on real-life occurrences, some names and identifying details have been changed to protect the privacy of individuals.

Introduction

Death: The Beginning
of Real Living

Death is so hard on the living. Some believe death is the ultimate defeat. I dare to disagree and often explain to my clients that I sometimes envy those who've crossed over because they are the ones who are truly living.

My own first taste of death came when I was just three years old and an older lady came to me in spirit to tell me that my grandma was going to die. I passed the message on to my mom, unknowing that dying was a horrible thing. The response that I received was a spanking. When my grandma passed just a few months later, and my predictions and communication with the Other Side was truer and real, my parents decided to enroll me early into the local Lutheran school. Not only would it keep me busy but they hoped that it would eradicate whatever demons that I was in communication with. To their dismay, I still saw, heard, knew, and sensed, but instead of expressing that I saw life after death, I stopped passing along the messages. I began to understand that what was normal for me wasn't normal for everyone.

I was surrounded by death, both by those so-called imaginary friends, who were talking to me, and by my mother's family, who was not faring well. My mom's oldest brother, Freeman McLaughlin, passed from cancer before I was born. Her youngest brother, Melvin, unexpectedly passed away from a heart attack when I was just a few years old. Soon afterward, my grandma passed.

My mom's dad, Grant McLaughlin, was a soft-spoken gentle giant who had a quick laugh. He was all my mom had left of her family, and he was also my favorite person in the world. After his sons passed away and then his wife, my grandfather became an even more notable fixture in our house, and a forever fixture in my heart. Just a few weeks before I was to enter the third grade, my grandfather was found next to his bed, badly beaten. Not long after his physical body died.

As they lowered the casket into the grave on that hot day in August, I saw him standing against a tree, smoking a cigarette. Excited and perhaps confused, I ran to him for a big hug. He confirmed in his gentle way that he was on his way to Heaven, but first he wanted to say his proper good-bye. He told me that he would always protect me and that I should never hesitate to call on him when I needed him. He confessed that he also could see, hear, feel, and communicate with the Other Side, just like I could. With a final hug, he walked toward the big, old crooked pine tree where his earthly body lay and disappeared. But not forever.

It wasn't long after my grandpa's funeral when I had a life-changing experience. While visiting a local mall with my parents, they set me on a bench with my book and told me to wait while they ran errands. Not long after they left, a man came up to me with a camera and asked to take my photograph. The lighting didn't seem to be right, according to him, and before I knew it the stranger was forcefully guiding me toward the exit of the mall. Before we got to the mall door, I could feel someone else standing over me and the would-be kidnapper. I knew it was my grandpa's energy, protecting me just as he said he would. I could smell his cigarette smoke, and I heard his voice yell for me to run. Then he reached between us and pushed me away from the man. Without hesitation, I ran as fast as I could toward the store my mom and dad were shopping in. Reports were made, but nobody was ever caught. During the same time period, there was an unidentified serial killer and some people thought he was the perpetrator. Whether it was him or just another bad guy, I know with all my heart and soul that my grandpa from the Other Side saved my life. My grandfather made a promise, and he kept it.

Although death had been in my life since I was the tender age of three, it wasn't until my grandpa's passing that it felt so final, despite my spirit connections. That was until he saved my life from the Other Side, and then it didn't feel so far away. I was being taught in my parochial schooling that Heaven was some far-off place, yet I was having connections in the here and now and the interaction with my grandpa proved to me that the Other Side was as close as a whisper.

It wasn't until I was close to thirty years old that I finally embraced what I called a curse for so long and realized it was truly a gift—a gift that everyone has. I'm not special, except that I work the psychic muscle more than maybe most. The sixth sense just needs to be recognized and unwrapped and then used.

I did the so-called normal thing of going to college, getting married to someone very much like the skeptical father I was raised by, having kids, getting divorced, and then getting married again. I did it differently with Chuck. He believed in all of me—the good, the bad, and the gift included. Chuck also had his own experiences with family and friends that he lost, experiences that weren't mere coincidences, but true signs. It's amazing what you can accomplish when you have that kind of support around you.

When my mom passed away in 2006, I felt like I was three years old all over again. I felt abandoned and like Heaven didn't exist. That dead was dead. Odd and a bit hypocritical, since my life purpose was to bridge this side to the other by being the telephone operator from Heaven to Earth. It was a series of communications from my mom that helped me through my own grief. It didn't remove the grief—I don't know if you ever get over a loss—even with the knowledge that they are not dead and living better than we are. It did, however, help me to walk through the grief with wider strides and wanting to help others on their own grief journeys.

Ways Heaven Says Hello

Just as we communicate differently with those on this earthly plane, it is the same for those on the Other Side. We also have to take into account that we don't change our personality when we cross over. So if your dad was a loudmouth on this side, he will be the same on the Other Side. If your mom was quiet and timid, it may take a bit more to catch her communication.

Communication with our loved ones comes in different forms, but typically it is through telepathy, clairaudience, and clairvoyance. Have you ever woken up to your name being called or saw a shadow out of the corner of your eye or just felt like you should take a different route instead of your normal one? More than likely that was a loved one trying to help you out or give you a Heaven hello. Here are some other ways Heaven says hello:

• You have a gut feeling.
• You have a shiver that goes down your spine.

- You feel an invisible touch that comforts you.
- Someone tells you information that you need at just the right time, and they know nothing that is going on in your life.
- You see repeated numbers or symbols or find coins.
- You are visited in nature by an animal or an insect in a way that there is no mistaking that it is a message.
- You see a shadow out of the corner of your eye.
- You see a presence, an outline of a person, or someone in the physical that reassembles them.
- You hear your name being called while sleeping or falling asleep.
- You hear a voice that sounds like your deceased loved one.
- You have electronic disturbances, such as a light bulb that keeps burning out or flickering or a cell phone that can't keep a charge.
- Smelling a familiar scent, such as a cigar, a flower, or perfume.

I'm often called as soon as a loved one passes. The pain and sadness are still fresh, and the person wants a connection to be made. They ask questions like: "Are they okay?" "Did they make it to the Other Side?" "What signs will they give me?" I often say to wait six to twelve months before visiting any medium, and for that I have the following reasons:

1. Your loved one needs to make their transition. Think of it as if they are at the airport waiting for their plane. Or they are on the plane to the Other Side and don't have phone service.
2. You have to grieve. Nobody knows how to grieve, but it's a process that just seems to happen.

3. They have to grieve. They have to get used to their surroundings without you, too. They have to get acclimated to the Other Side, just as you have to get used to them not being here in the physical.

4. They have to unpack and find their place. Think of it as if they've reached their destination, have to find their new home, reunite with loved ones they haven't seen in a while (maybe even reconcile), and figure out what's next for them in their new world.

5. They have to hook up their "phone." Not a true and real phone, but just as we all have our own way of communicating here, they do there also. Some say they wish there were visiting hours in Heaven—there is, but you just have to give it time and have patience.

We all receive Heaven hellos from our loved ones, but life happens and we become consumed by it, missing what may come in a subtle way. My hope is that by becoming aware of the different signs I outline in the following pages that you can find your signs. Then the visiting hours with your loved ones on the Other Side will become more frequent and clearer.

Chapter One

The Beginning

The finality of death is what makes so many afraid of what they seem to believe is the end. But do we close our eyes and no longer exist or do we close our eyes and open them to another life?

Misunderstood

Not everyone understands how, why, or when I see spirit. Most of the time I don't either. It's like asking a music prodigy why he or she is good at piano and how do they do it. They just do. Some days are easier than others, in both the connections and the emotional exhaustion that comes from the so-called job. Oftentimes the misunderstanding of the connection creates fear.

One of the reasons I didn't want to be a professional psychic medium was because of the crazy reputation the label has. I grew up during the Psychic Friend's Network and Ms. Cleo era. I don't wear long, flowing gowns—I'm too short and will trip if I tried—and I don't burn incense, instead I prefer Yankee Candles. Although society has branched out thanks to some television shows, there are still many who misunderstand psychics, mediums, and the connections to the Other Side. Many just don't really want to understand anything different from what they were raised with.

When I started doing readings for a popular radio show smack-dab in the middle of the Bible Belt, I was told that I was crazy, but ironically I didn't have any problems. I did a popular bimonthly call-in segment with the radio station for several years. I had a different experience in 2015 when I released *It's a Wonderful Afterlife*. That October, a paper did a front-page story that promoted a local library event I was to have to speak and promote the book. The paper was delivered to thousands of residents in the area of Macomb County, Michigan. As soon as it was released, I began to receive death threats from a group of men who promised to douse me with gasoline and set me on fire.

The threats were taken seriously by law enforcement, and I was gifted an escort to the small Michigan suburban library that I'd been visiting for years. Typically speakers had an audience of a hundred, but close to five hundred people turned out for this lecture, many of them had to be turned away due to lack of room. I joked to one of the officers that they were just looking forward to possibly seeing the Shelby Township Psychic Trial, like the Salem Witch Trial. He grinned back and said that he believed it was that they just wanted to learn more about what is considered taboo—death and the afterlife. It was obvious that the topic of the afterlife and loss of a loved one hit home for many, since after the program the line wound around the building as I signed books and thanked the people for their support.

I didn't go up in flames that night, thankfully. Instead, a community shared their own stories of Heaven hellos and were grateful to know that they weren't alone.

We All Have the Gift

We are all given the gift of signs from our loved ones on the Other Side. The amazing thing is that they vary, just like the personalities of the people you lost. Objects move, you might receive an invisible touch, or a bird often visits your windowsill. You may find a note written years ago that appears at the right time, or get an odd text message. You may be awakened and see your loved one standing over you or dream about them sitting on a beach in a tropical island. There's no right sign or wrong sign, but there are missed signs, mostly due to overanalyzing the situation or chalking it up to your imagination. The signs will come more often when you recognize them. Our loved ones on the Other Side want us to know that they are at peace in the afterlife.

The Blessing

I've seen, heard, and communicated with spirits since I was a toddler, and I have dedicated my life to bridging the connection to this world and the Other Side through sessions, lectures, and books like this one. Although not everybody understands what I do, or even accepts what I do, it's a calling. I honestly thought I'd be a prosecuting attorney, a social worker, or a psychologist—psychic medium wasn't at all on my radar. It didn't help that I attended parochial school and had pretty conservative Lutheran parents who believed that anybody who saw, heard, or communicated with the Other Side had a direct link to the devil. In order to tame my constant talk of *imaginary friends,* my parents enrolled me in parochial school. If our religion believed in the power of holy water, they may have thrown that in too, instead Lutheran school had to do.

Being raised with the teachings of the Lutheran belief and being told continually through church, school, and Sunday school that anything to do with psychics, mediums, spirits, and ghosts was evil and unacceptable put my already low self-esteem at rock bottom. Was I evil? I didn't feel that way! I fought with the rationale, my sanity, and my religion. It wasn't until I was in my twenties that I decided to consult my pastor, a conservative Missouri Synod Lutheran.

I sat down across from the pastor, not quite sure how to begin. His eyes looked into mine with confusion. I had never asked to meet with him before, and my call to the church secretary probably sounded urgent. I was the goody-goody type girl, an honor role student in high school, active in youth groups, the choir, the band, drama, varsity sports—an all-American girl. I married a man who was also very all-American, and we had two precious young children; we were looked upon as the all-American family. Just the weekend before, my {then} husband and I were at a local store and were stopped by a parishioner who commented on what a beautiful family we made. There are always closed doors and there are always skeletons, and I felt the need to confess mine.

Marital problems were my real reason for the appointment. I married a skeptic, so I tried to put away the abilities, but the issues became severe. It was as if Pandora's box opened up and I was being literally and figuratively haunted. The marital problems and the psychic problems had all been hidden, so the reason why I was sitting across from the minister, wringing my hands profusely, confused him.

Not necessarily knowing how to begin, I merely blurted out that I was able to see ghosts, angels, and spirits. And they all spoke to me. My minister looked at me without expression and asked me to explain more in-depth the degree of communication. I was certain he thought I'd lost my mind, but then his son on the Other Side came through.

I told him that his son was appearing to me at that moment. I whispered, "He said he drowned, Pastor. He shows me water in his lungs. He also says that it wasn't your fault."

His son looked all of four years old, but he spoke intelligently and clearly. I looked from my pastor to his little boy and back again. Tears ran down his face, but he didn't wipe them away, he only looked at me strangely.

Here it goes, I thought. *This is when I'm given my excommunication from the church.* I had a tendency to believe the worst and never the better (things have since changed).

"Kristy, what else does he say?"

"He said that he watches over your daughter—his sister—and his niece. He's so honored that she was named after him. And he says that he loves that you buy an ornament in his memory every year, even though his mom thinks it is silly."

"Nobody knows that but my family. I've never talked about Samuel or his passing. Or that Diane named Samantha after her brother. That's—" He shook his head in confusion. "That's just mind-boggling. Do you know that he passed on my watch, Kristy? Elaine was at a women's conference and I was watching him, but I became consumed in preparing for the next day's service. Before I knew it, he had disappeared."

"He said he was always curious, and he was a bit autistic. He loved water."

My pastor nodded in agreement. "We never had an official diagnosis, and we were talking about seeking a specialist because he was smart—wow was he smart—but there were developmental problems. He loved water. I was waiting until the next summer to take that pool down."

The words caught in the pastor's throat, and he held his bowed head in his hands and sobbed. I wasn't sure what to do. Should I comfort him? Should I continue the dialogue between his son to him? Before I could make a decision, the pastor looked up at me with tears still shining in his eyes, and he asked me to pray with him. I obliged.

Sam was his son who nobody in the parish knew existed. He had drowned in the family pool more than thirty years before, way before the pastor accepted his calling to my church. After we prayed, he gave me a hug and then his blessing to pursue the work he believed was given to me by God. Happily ever after, right? Nope. A theology debate with me playing devil's advocate took place over plenty of counseling sessions. He told me that it wouldn't be easy, me being who I was, but that if it were easy everybody would do it.

"Even in the Bible the people were afraid of the unknown; afraid of the spirit life," he'd said, "but Jesus continued to prove that the spirit life existed and continues to exist."

The week before he passed away, just a few weeks after being diagnosed with cancer, we had one last visit. "You didn't choose to be a psychic, Kristy. God bestowed that gift upon you with your free choice to use it or ignore it. I hope you use it, because I'd love to check up on you when I get across the pearly gate."

A few months after his funeral, I was sitting in my new office waiting for my next client when I heard a buzzing, as if a fly had found its way inside. It was then that my pastor appeared, hand in hand with his little boy named Sam. No words were said; he simply smiled and disappeared.

I felt blessed beyond words, and still do.

Chapter Two

You Didn't Come

Natalie came to see me about six months after her mom passed away. Natalie and her mom had a turbulent relationship from the get go. Both were strong-willed and hardheaded women; if Natalie said blue, her mom would say green, and if her mom said red, Natalie would say dark red. They were oil and water. Although they loved one another, it was simply a toxic relationship. It was so toxic that her siblings didn't tell her of her mother's death until the day after she passed.

Just as soon as Natalie sat down across from me, her mom came through in spirit. There was no denying it was her mother either because they looked like identical twins, all the way down to the wrinkles. Her mom stood there, glaring.

"She's not happy," I shared, concerned Natalie would be mad at me. My sessions were supposed to be healing, and this one wasn't starting out that way.

"She never was," Natalie said tartly.

Her mother, alert and even more fired up, spouted, "She didn't even come to my funeral, of course I'm mad! I'm pissed. I'm her mother, and she didn't pay me respect in life and now not even in death."

"Why didn't you go to your mother's funeral?" I asked. "She's hurt by it."

Natalie's mom glared at me for rearranging her message.

"Isn't she dead? How would she know that I wasn't there? And why would she care? She didn't care to have me around in life." Natalie's tough exterior began to shed and her brown eyes watered.

"Not true. Not true at all!" the spirit yelled. "I would jump in front of a bus for that girl." She looked at her daughter, who was trying to gain her composure, and in a softer voice added, "I would, too. I really would."

I believed her, and when I shared the message with Natalie I knew she believed it, too.

Natalie shared that her siblings had made her feel like an outcast. If she had gone to the funeral she was sure there'd have been a fight. "They want her money and they want my share, too. It's okay, they can have it. I just wish I'd had my good-bye."

Natalie's mom looked sullen, but I could tell she knew there was truth to Natalie's words. "Tell her there is money. Not a lot, but there's a trust in each kid's name and nobody else can touch the other's money. So the joke is on them. Go buy yourself a condo, Nat. I'm so sorry for everything."

Natalie's mom disappeared.

"You must be mistaken, Kristy. There's no money. I would've heard about it by now. But most importantly, tell my mom that I'm sorry too."

"I think she knows that. Her showing up was the white flag I wish you had found when she was still here. As for the money, it's there, but I think you need to approach that carefully with your siblings. Maybe ask your mom to help arrange for some healing on that part, too."

"She can do that from the Other Side?"

"Absolutely!"

Four months later, right before Christmas, I received a card in the mail with a note from Natalie.

"You were right. Or Mom was. My oldest sister reached out to me and asked me over for Thanksgiving dinner, and I accepted. I was grateful for the olive branch. After dinner she handed me the paperwork to collect my portion of Mom's trust. I know that Mom arranged for it all. Thank you!"

Go to the Funeral

"She's passed away," I sobbed into the phone.

"I'm so sorry. I will try and get to the funeral, but Billy has a lot of homework and my mom needs to go to the grocery store."

I hadn't even told her when my mother's funeral was and the person who was supposed to be my best friend was already making excuses not to go. I was numb and I didn't like confrontation, so I mumbled something about having to finish the funeral arrangements and hung up.

My lesson on attending funerals was learned when I was only five years old and my beloved school principal passed away. A huge funeral was planned, with all the school kids having to sing at it.

"I don't want to go, Mom," I remember saying. Not just because it was a funeral, but because of my heightened empath abilities. Since I was three years old I had been able to see and communicate with those on the Other Side, but the difficult part was feeling everyone's emotions.

Just a year before my grandma passed away, so did my uncle. Funerals were becoming all too frequent in my young life.

"You go to pay your respects—not to the person who died, but to show support to those still here," my mom explained.

I wasn't excited about the explanation. I was too young to understand at the time that it was also hard on my mom. To be blunt, I was not a compassionate person, especially with my mom, but she wasn't easy to get along with either. In the end, I realized that we were very similar, right down to the empathic qualities. The difference was she didn't understand her psychic gift and her sensitivity turned to deep depression and unexplained physical ailments. So I didn't realize how hard it was for her to tell me that I had to go to a funeral and for her to walk into the church while holding my hand, too. I know now.

That funeral was more than forty years ago, but I still remember the look on the face of the principal's wife when she saw all the schoolchildren were there. It was a bit of joy she was able to get in an overall gloomy time.

I never knew how similar planning a funeral was to planning a wedding. The clothes, the music, the scriptures, the program … it all had to be perfect. My mom loved flowers and my sister and I went to the florist together and carefully chose each stem for her casket arrangement.

"Nobody will come to my funeral," my mom would say. "Nobody visited me in life, why would they do it in death? They shouldn't! Spend the time while they are living, Kristy."

I would then remind her of her own wisdom. "Mom, funerals are for the living!"

My mom would only smirk in response.

But it was true. During my mother's funeral, the funeral home was filled with family and friends of the family. When my ex in-laws came, I cried. They had been a part of my life since my early teens and a divorce didn't divorce me from them. They were Mom and Dad to me as well.

The night before Mom's funeral, I received a text from my best friend saying that she wouldn't be there because her mom needed to go grocery shopping—she was sorry. I still remember being in the middle of the men's department at JcPenney looking for a shirt for my dad when the text came through. I simply shut my eyes and squeezed the tears away. I did the same when my ex-husband didn't come to say good-bye to my mom. I wasn't sad for me, but for my kids—our kids.

Communication stopped with my friend after the funeral no-show, but not from my doing. It just stopped. When I received word that her mom passed, I went to the funeral because I was taught that was what you did. I never heard from her after.

Nobody likes funerals, but my mama was right—you do what you have to do because it's the right thing, not necessarily the fun thing. You go to funerals for closure and to say good-bye, to comfort the living, and even to say your peace. I went to one funeral where everybody had to stand up and share a funny story of the deceased. Afterward, the family had a party. Not a reception, a party. Everybody mourns differently. Some would rather grieve in private. I attended one send-off where only a few select friends and family were invited and we all sat and crocheted in silence, with her urn sitting center stage on the table. It was a hobby that she loved to do, often crocheting scarves for the homeless, and we thought it would be something she'd love. So we crocheted for Dottie.

There's no right or wrong way to grieve or pay your respects. It is simply what feels right in your heart. Do that.

My Other Dad

It was a warm September afternoon when I met my future father-in-law as he picked up his son from school. It was his birthday and he bought himself a silver Mercury Cougar that he was especially giddy about. I didn't know at that moment the future impact he would have on my life and on the lives of those around me.

Five years later I married his son, we had two beautiful children, and eight years after that his son and I divorced. Despite the divorce, my {ex} in-laws continued to be Mom and Dad to me, and the best grandparents one could ever wish for to our children. Blood was thicker than water, but their grandchildren shared my blood too, so we continued a relationship with mutual respect and a love that stayed constant.

On September 21, 2014, hours before the autumn equinox, after a long and brave battle, my {ex} father-in-law crossed over into Heaven. His passing affected me more than I thought it would. I thought I was prepared, but after receiving the news over the phone from my daughter, who had just days before moved more than eight hundred miles away, I realized that you can never really be prepared. Even expected passings can feel totally unexpected.

I came home from my office and sat on the couch, numb, mulling over memories, mistakes, and misfortunes, and trying to remember the last time I saw him. Did I give him a hug? Did he know how much I cared about him? Did he even care to know? Did he remember the argument we had when I was just a teenager because he wanted to fast-forward through to a movie and I wanted to watch the previews? That was the only argument we ever had, but thirty-something years later I'd always regretted the silliness of it. Did he know how much I valued that he and his wife came to almost every single school function for both my daughter and my son, even when you could tell that he wasn't feeling well? And did he know that the Sunday morning tradition of taking the kids to church and then to breakfast would never be the same without Chuck, my {now} husband, teasingly calling out to the kids, "Grandpa's here with the church bus!"?

And then I felt guilty for grieving. Yes, guilty. He wasn't my father-in-law anymore. What right did I have to grieve? How could I put a label on how I felt? I couldn't, yet I cried anyway, ignoring the phone calls, the text messages, and the computer. I just lay down right where I was and stared through the kaleidoscope of tears until I fell asleep. I woke up to Chuck laying a blanket over me and gently touching my hair. As if reading my mind, he simply said, "You're allowed to be sad. I'm sad. He was a part of your life, both directly and indirectly. He's your kids' grandpa." And the waterworks fell once more.

"I don't think I can go to the funeral," I told Chuck. "I don't belong. No, I don't know *where* I belong," I said.

Before Chuck could answer, I heard my mom's voice in my head say, "You go to the funeral, Kristy. You go to the funeral." And so I did.

Photos from throughout the years were pinned to photo boards in the narthex of the church. I stopped to gaze at one photo, his arm around me and both of us laughing at more than likely something silly he had said. Even though I didn't share his last name anymore, he had been an important part of my life, and not even divorce could remove the carefully engraved memories of him within my heart. As the family, including my kids, took their place at the front of the church, Chuck and I found a seat toward the back.

The church was filled with relatives and friends. Many people I hadn't seen since my wedding to the kids' dad more than thirty years before. The service was touching, with even the minister breaking down and crying as he shared touching stories of the man I had never told how much he meant to me. Chuck wiped away his own tears and squeezed my hand in support.

After the service, our ride home was quiet, until I heard my mom telepathically tell me she was proud of me for going to the funeral. I was glad she taught me well.

Instant Grieving

Within hours of the announcement of my {ex} father-in-law's passing, I began to receive the insensitive comments. I wondered if we are in that much of an instant society that even grieving was supposed to be instant, too.

Some comments that I received included:

- You're a medium. You get to see him anytime. Why are you upset?
- Maybe you need antidepressants.
- You still have your father, what's the big deal?
- I'm sorry for your loss, but can you come over tonight to do readings at my party?

Everyone grieves differently. I see it every day, all day long, in my office. The interesting thing I have learned about grief is that everyone really does it in their own time and in their own way. Don't just expect people to "get over it" because it's convenient for you, and don't expect others to understand your grieving either, because it's a personal experience.

No person has the right to condemn you on how you repair your heart or how you choose to grieve, because no one knows how much you're hurting. Recovering from a loss takes time and everyone heals at their own pace, in their own time. The corporate three days policy doesn't mean that the person is over it in three days. When my mom passed away, I was in planning mode and never got the time to grieve. It was ten months later when it all hit me. There is no normal when it comes to grief. You are allowed to grieve and go through the myriad of emotions. And it may be twenty years after the passing when the memories and missing come flooding back all over again, and the grief process starts at the very beginning.

We aren't given a manual on how to grieve or how to help someone grieve, and even if there is one, it's hardly the beach read anyone wants to do. The empathic side of most humans wants to take the hurt away, or to run away from the hurt. Some people are better at giving comfort and love than others, but no matter your personality and experiences there are ways to offer support.

WHAT NOT TO SAY TO SOMEONE GRIEVING

- He/She is in a better place.
- You are so strong!
- There's a reason for this, you know.
- Well, he/she was old.
- At least he/she lived as long as they did.
- I know how you feel.

WHAT TO SAY TO SOMEONE GRIEVING

- I'm sorry for your loss.
- Do you want to talk about it?
- Would you like to go out for coffee?
- Is there anything I can help you with?

WHAT NOT TO DO

- Rationalize the death.
- Be judgmental about the death.
- Be judgmental about the mourners.
- Put a time frame on mourning.
- Ignore the loss.

WHAT DO TO

- Be supportive.
- Don't ask for anything immediately.
- Allow the person who is grieving to mourn.
- Don't put a time limit on mourning.
- Keep the support going even after the funeral.

I may be a medium, and I am gifted with the ability to see, sense, and hear from loved ones on the Other Side (as we all are), but I'm not Samantha from *Bewitched*. I can't wiggle my nose and make them appear when I want. And, as I say in my office every day, we are physical beings and it is natural and normal to miss and want that physical being with us. Yes, we can draw comfort from the signs and our visits, but it isn't the same as the physical presence—even for me.

If you offer support and love and receive an iced response, it could be that the person grieving is simply having a hard time taking his/her guard down. The most important thing you can do for a grieving person is to simply be there.

F. Scott Fitzgerald's quote that says "Life starts all over again when it gets crisp in the fall" has a new meaning for me and my family during September. The time is often called "the wintering," where you put your summer clothes away, get the winter sweaters and wool blankets from storage, and fill your pantry with canned goods. It's a time where you are supposed to look over your year's harvest and make amendments for next year. It's a time when the blooms die and stay dormant until new blooms again appear. But some of the blooms won't appear the same way that they did. They lived out their time. Sometimes the blooms will stay as mere memories that simply have to be held on to. It doesn't mean the blooms are any less beautiful, just different.

Remember that blooms will again appear after a loss, but don't spend time wishing for what is to come or what should've been and miss what is right now. And go to the funeral. It may be a tough thing, but it's the right thing.

Chapter Three

Signs

It is natural to want to contact a lost loved one, especially when it is a sudden passing, but after more than fifteen years of professionally doing readings and making contact with spirits for more than forty years, I've come to find that a year after the transition seems to be a good timeline before visiting any medium. Now if you ask twenty other mediums, you will probably get twenty different answers, and beware of those who say to come right in. More times than not, in those cases the medium simply wants to take advantage of the newly bereaved. I suggest taking your time when seeking a medium for the connection. Not only do you have to get used to your loved one not being here in the physical but they also have to adjust to their new universe. The process of grief and the emotions that come from it should be as balanced as they can be in order to get a clear connection. That goes for seeing your own sign without the help of a medium. It doesn't mean that the communication can't happen, because there are always exceptions.

It's common to want to find out if they are alright. Here in this world of instant gratification we are gifted with the ability of a quick connection. We ask for our loved ones to text or call us once they've reached their destination, but that doesn't always work that way in the next world, unfortunately.

Many people discount their experiences, thinking that they are just imagining it, yet we often receive these Heaven hellos when we most need them. These heavenly occurrences can happen any-where—home, work, the funeral home, on a trip, in a car, in a de-partment store—at any time of day or night. But we are so often stressed out that we miss them.

Why the Signs?

Our loved ones want to reassure us that they've landed safely on the Other Side.

What Does It All Mean?

I've had numerous clients contact me after receiving a sign. Many think the worst and fear that the interaction is a warning or that their loved one is in distress, when most of the time our loved ones on the Other Side just want to offer a reassuring message. It re-quires you to interpret what is happening in your world as to what their message might mean at that time. Some of the most frequent messages are quite simple and they include:

- I'm okay.
- Please don't worry about me.
- I'm concerned that you are so stressed out.
- Please forgive me.
- Please don't feel guilty.
- You need to go on with your life.
- We will be together again.

• I will always love you.

• I do hear you when you talk to me.

A sign should bring you peace. Whether it is the feather that you keep finding or a dream that you had with your passed loved one, you should feel a sense of healing. If it's bringing you anxiety and stress, it's best to look within your own heart and soul to see why. The missing is normal, but you should still feel a sense of contentment.

The next time you are missing someone special or feeling especially frustrated and stressed, take a minute to look around and notice what may seem like mere coincidences. More than likely you are being sent love from the Other Side.

I Want a Sign Now

"It's been three months, Kristy, and my husband still hasn't given me a sign. Has he made it to Heaven or is he ... ?"

Debbie was a new client who told me immediately upon meeting me that she was a skeptic. I was good with skeptics, I just asked that there be honesty and openness during the sessions.

I saw Debbie's husband, Ralph, standing right beside her, holding Easter lilies. He wore a look of concern and sadness that I was trying to interpret.

"Debbie, he's holding potted Easter lilies. Do you know what that means?"

Debbie laughed and nodded her head in understanding.

"Tell her that the lilies spread, and she kills the roses," Ralph said, his energy lightening up a bit.

I repeated what Ralph said and Debbie laughed again, but she didn't verbally validate or expand on the message.

"Tell her that I've come through to her several times, but she's too hardheaded to connect the dots. Let her know I will always bring her lilies."

Ralph's energy once again turned melancholy, and I realized that he was worried she was mad at him. Not only had he not been gone for long, but he was like a little boy with his hand caught in a cookie jar, worried about his punishment. Not the judgment in a religious sense, but the repercussions from hurting his own wife.

It had only been three months since his passing and three months was just too soon for her to have an appointment with me. Ironically, she had booked her appointment a year ago, before Ralph passed. He told me that he hadn't been taking care of himself, and although he knew he had diabetes, had high blood pressure, and was overweight, he also thought himself immortal and ate and drank what he wanted. He just plain didn't take good care of himself. So maybe the cookie jar wasn't simply an analogy.

"You're sure he isn't in Hell?" Debbie asked, wiping her eyes with a tissue.

"Positive," I said. "I don't have Hell on speed dial," I joked.

"Why is she asking me that?" I asked Ralph in my head. "Why would she think you are in Hell?"

Ralph then informed me that they loved watching the paranormal and psychic shows. "If there isn't a sign, the shows said the loved one either didn't cross over to Heaven or went to the other place."

I groaned. When one popular fiction show came out in the mid-2000s, I was inundated with e-mails and calls from people petrified that their loved ones were stuck, or earthbound, because of unfinished business. "Don't we all have unfinished business?" I would respond. It's rare that someone becomes earthbound, although I have witnessed it, and I've helped the spirit find their way into the light. And as for Hell, well, I was telling Debbie the truth. It wasn't a location that I wanted to make a connection to. No, Ralph had transitioned, but they were both too hardheaded to communicate. I had a feeling this was the same way their marriage had been when he was here.

"He thinks you're mad at him, Debbie. He thinks you're disappointed in him, so as soon as he steps forward where you might be able to sense him or receive a sign from him, he turns and backs away. He's afraid of your reaction."

"As he should be," Debbie yelled, throwing the tissue box across the room. "He left me with a mess. He left me with a financial mess, and he left me. He should be afraid. He left me," she screamed. Her voice caught and her anger turned to sobs.

I got out of my chair and did what I've done numerous times with other clients, I let Debbie sob into my shoulder.

"You are allowed to be mad," I said quietly.

"I don't want to be, though," she said, composing herself. "I loved him, and he promised he'd be with me forever. And now he isn't."

"It's true. He isn't here in the physical, but he will be with you forever from the Other Side."

I looked over at Ralph, who looked uncomfortable. I could tell he was a man who wasn't good with emotions, and that hadn't changed with his transition.

"I want my sign now, though," she sniffled.

"Give Ralph some time, Debbie. Give yourself some time. I promise, you'll receive that sign when you least expect it but when you most need it."

She wasn't exactly thrilled that I couldn't wave a magic wand and produce an instant sign, but I knew that what was shared would make sense later. I just didn't know when or how.

Six months later, Debbie showed up at my office with her daughter, who had an appointment.

"I have to show you this, Kristy," Debbie said, scrolling through the photos in her phone. "See this?"

I looked at her screen and saw a photo of a lily growing out of a crack in a sidewalk. I curiously nodded.

"I stepped outside my side door one morning and it had grown in a crack in the drive. There are no lilies anywhere around. I think that's what he meant when he showed you lilies. Well, that and on our first date he didn't give me a rose, instead he gave me a potted lily plant."

I groaned at her late validation.

"Oh, and one more thing," she said, swiping her phone screen again to a photo of a baby girl. "This is our newest grandbaby. My son and his wife had been waiting years on an adoption and out of the blue she became available. Guess what the birth mother had named her?"

"Lily," I grinned.

"I'm still mad at him, but I also feel like he's trying, something he didn't do so much on Earth." Debbie thought for a moment and added, "Or maybe he did and I didn't notice. I wish I'd noticed more like I am now."

Don't become obsessed with receiving a sign or the lack of receiving a sign. The old saying that a watched pot never boils is apropos for signs as well. Often you are receiving your signs, but you are looking in the wrong direction. Years ago, I was conducting a paranormal investigation with a group at an old mansion. The group laid all of their equipment out on the table and was intently staring at it, awaiting any fluctuations. In the meantime, standing behind them was a couple in spirit who had passed away from a tragic fire. I couldn't help but laugh at the sight. Who was hunting who, I joked later, after I pointed out the odd shadows on the wall that their energy created. No instruments were going to pick that up, only patience and an open perception.

Love from the Other Side

The signs that we get from the Other Side are as different as the people we've loved and lost. While Dad might constantly knock down the picture you have displayed of him on your armoire, Mom might send you dimes that you find in the oddest places. There's no hard and fast rule as to what they can and can't do in order to show their love from the Other Side.

It's All in the Vibe

By opening yourself up to helping others, you also open yourself up to communication with the Other Side. It's all about vibration. The more joyful and loving you feel, the more of those situations you attract.

We are each born with our own individual vibration that sends signals out to others of like vibrations. Those signals either attract or dismiss situations, events, and even people. As we go through life experiences, both good and bad, we sometimes become out of sync with our unique signal, such as a radio between stations. The signal is strong when we move into a harmonic place, but once we allow fears or negativity to invade, the signal is reduced. It is deafening to the spirit when the vibration is in its white noise phase, and those between stations may find themselves sad, frustrated, and depressed.

Have you ever started talking to a complete stranger while waiting in the checkout line and after just seconds you decided that you really liked that person? Or have you ever gone to a party and been introduced to someone who you just didn't like right off the bat? You were tuning in to vibration. You had no reason to like or not like them other than an instant impression, which was actually a sensing of vibration.

If your vibration is different from another, you may rub one another the wrong way. Although the vibration is sensed and not notably obvious from a physical standpoint, you may not realize that it is affecting things, such as your employment chances. By not being tuned in to who you are, or simply creating a facade, you may be attracting the lack in your life that you don't want and breaking your connection to the Other Side. It is that same vibration that helps tune us in to our loved ones on the Other Side. Or untune us from our loved ones on the Other Side.

Wear Bright Clothes
Colors enhance and minimize your vibration by changing your aura. Most people wear black, gray, or brown clothing, especially in the winter, but these colors actually mute your vibration and decrease the actual perception you want to reflect. By adding color to your wardrobe, you shift your mood and the moods of those around you, and you also showcase your uniqueness. Just as our loved ones on the Other Side try to send us signs that they are around in a vivid way—the bright yellow butterfly, the red cardinal, the purple flower, etc.—we need to align ourselves in that same vibration.

Sing
Whether in the shower or in the car, singing helps to realign your vibration, make you happy, and even make you laugh. I would suggest that if you use mass transit you skip this one, especially if your

singing voice isn't appealing, as it may cause the opposite effect to those around you. All kidding aside, even if you can't carry a tune or you don't sound like Adele, singing lifts you to a higher vibration.

Exercise

Besides the obvious positive reasons for exercise, moving your body actually raises your vibration and helps you connect to the now.

Eat Healthy

We feel good when we eat healthy. Simple, right? Not only do healthy foods make us feel good, it resets the vibration. By choosing to eat foods the colors of a rainbow, you realign the chakras within your energy field.

Creativity

It doesn't matter what creative project you decide to do, just do something creative—paint, color in a coloring book, or even garden. By adding creativity to your life, it helps to rebalance you, which will help you think clearer and come up with brighter (pun intended) ideas for your life.

Goals

We often lose sight of our goals when the vibrational knob is between stations, so it is important to write down at least ten goals, post them where you see them daily, and work on completing them. It helps you clearly articulate from your heart and soul what you want.

Love Yourself

Write down ten things about yourself that show you are a good person. Reminding yourself of your positive qualities accentuates your vibration to those here and those on the Other Side.

Declutter Your Life

Chaos breeds chaos. Declutter your car, your closet, your Facebook, etc. The less you have to carry around emotionally, the easier it is to realign your vibration.

Sleep

Lack of sleep can cause all sorts of issues—mentally, physically, and psychically. Although you want to get enough sleep before your reading with a medium, it is also important to make this your routine.

Passion

Pursue a passion, whether it is playing piano or taking photos. Stop with the excuses of money, time, or fear—just do it!

Intuition

Pay very close attention to your intuition. How do you feel? How does your body feel? What are the thoughts in your mind? The more you pay attention to those gut feelings, the more you will be able to make positive changes in your life.

Surround Yourself with Positive People

By surrounding yourself with positive people, you expand and grow yourself and attract more of the same.

Pay It Forward

It will get good energy flowing for you, and you'll gain perspective.

Relax, Let Go, and Smile

Relax and let go. Write a letter to your guides/angels if you can't relax. Meditate. Take a yoga class. Start breathing again. Practice letting go and being mindful of the now.

Is This Good-Bye?

Nathan Martins was always traveling. It was simply part of his job, and his wife knew that before they even married. It didn't mean that she liked it, though. It wasn't that Andrea didn't trust Nathan, it was that she always had this sinking feeling in her stomach each time he left for a long trip.

"You're being silly," Nathan would tell her, always with a kiss. "You know that I always come back. This isn't good-bye!"

As much as Nathan tried to reassure Andrea, she couldn't shake the anxiety. It became so bad that she went to her doctor for medication. Although it took the edge off, she still had that nagging feeling.

It was June 2015 when her intuition turned into reality, and the phone call came that her husband had been traveling on the freeway when a truck tire blew and flew over the freeway into oncoming traffic. Nathan tried to avoid the debris but couldn't, and he died instantly.

The funeral was surreal. She sat with their four teenagers, all of them numb to the fact that he wouldn't be walking in the door with his crooked smile and infectious laughter.

Andrea had made an appointment with me the year before, specifically to speak to her mom, never imagining that instead her appointment would fall just one day after her husband's funeral.

When Andrea sat down, she was surrounded by loved ones. Front and center was a handsome man who showed me his wedding ring, a sign for me that it's a spouse.

"There's a man here who says he loves you very much, and that you were right, he should've listened. He's sorry."

Andrea began to cry.

"Although he wishes he were here, he wants you to know that it isn't good-bye."

Andrea looked up at me and asked me to repeat myself.

"He says this isn't good-bye, it's a different kind of hello."

It was what he said after every conversation on the phone, and every time he walked out the door on his travels. Even in the afterlife he was letting her know he would be around.

A couple months after Nathan crossed over, Andrea was having a particularly difficult day when a truck pulled in front of her on the way to get lunch. Swearing, she slammed on her brakes, stopping just inches from the truck's bumper. Right in front of her was the license plate that said HELLO NM. Her sign and Nathan's initials.

We are all able to make our own connection. You don't need me or another medium. You simply need to tune out, tune in, and see *your* hello.

I Heart You

"The one person who should have loved me no matter what didn't think I was worth the fight. She didn't think I was worth any love, and I don't want to give her the time now."

The lady in spirit hung her head in shame as her daughter explained their tumultuous relationship. "It's true, I did everything wrong. She's right. After Cara's father left me, my best friend was alcohol. I hurt so badly, and I couldn't stop. Okay, I didn't want to stop and feel."

"Excuses," Cara cried. "She was always filled with excuses! Wasn't I worth more than the bottle? I felt like an outsider in my own family!"

"My drinking was suicide, and I know that now. Please tell her I'm sorry," Cara's mom said and then disappeared.

"Is she just sorry for herself or for what she did to me and all who loved her and wanted to be loved by her?" she asked me between sobs.

It was a question I couldn't answer, but I knew what she felt like. I had not been in her exact situation, but we've all felt like the outsider, haven't we? It hurts. Many times there isn't an explanation, and we're left with a lot of pain that needs to be released.

I grew up in Detroit. I saw and communicated with spirits. I went to a Lutheran school where that wasn't accepted, nor was it accepted in my own home. I was an introvert and horribly shy. I had a sick Mom. Oh, I could go on and on, just as we all could, but what it came down to was I felt alone. I felt like an outsider, yet not even knowing what the inside was or who was graced to be in the in crowd.

I remember my parents taking me to a new church in a wealthy suburb. As they went to Bible study they had me go to Sunday school—something I admit I didn't like no matter which church, but especially in a new place. When the teacher asked me to state my name and where I lived, I answered Detroit, and the class erupted into laughs, including the leader. I was mortified and ran out, hiding in the bathroom until it was time to meet my parents. That moment was just one in a million times where I felt like an outsider. I was never embarrassed or ashamed about who I was or where I lived or who my parents were, though. And none of those examples of feeling on the outside changed me; instead they helped me understand myself and others. It wasn't until later in life that I realized being an outsider wasn't a bad thing. I just had to let go of what was expected. It hurts to let go. Sometimes it seems the harder you try to hold on to something or someone the more it tries to get away. That is when you have to move through and stop avoiding it.

"Your mom shows me a heart, Cara. I'm not sure if it's symbolic or a true and real heart."

The Other Side loves to share big and bright messages, such as light, rainbows, and hearts.

Cara looked at me sideways for a moment. "Mom never said she loved me, she always said she hearted me. After she passed, I began finding objects in the shape of hearts. Here, let me show you," Cara pulled out her cell phone and began to swipe through various pictures of stones shaped like hearts, a heart earring she found on her front walk, a ray of sunshine that was in the shape of a heart, and more than thirty other various heart-shaped objects.

"And you don't think that's a sign?" I smiled.

Cara came back to see me about two years later.

"Is my mom here?"

I nodded.

"I'd like to talk to her now. I realized that I was becoming her, just without the alcohol. I was avoiding, or trying to avoid, my life scars and hers, too. I think she was trying to tell me to open my heart."

"She says she's still sending you hearts, and she always will."

Cara smiled bright.

Cara didn't forget. Instead, she gave herself time to pause and contemplate. It was then she was able to conquer and come to terms with what happened. It helped her move through and move on.

Do you feel like the outsider? It's okay to be different. It's okay to have scars. It's okay to be comfortable in your own skin. It's okay to let go of past anger. It's okay for you to have desires. It's okay to be an outsider. After all, we're the ones who get the fresh air. The rain sometimes too, but the storms pass and we get rainbows, or in Cara's case hearts, as a reward.

I know so many of you who have hurt hearts and the voice within you saying you don't have any strength left to keep going. I've been there—face-planted in the carpet, soaked with tears and a hurt heart that burned. You might be thinking of giving up and giving in. I'm telling you that it can be okay. That you are worth it.

Being on the outside isn't a bad thing at all, because there are other outsiders to help bring comfort and who understand. You have to focus on you and invest in people and situations worth investing in. When you feel especially lost, keep telling yourself that it's not your monkeys and not your circus and to stop entertaining the clowns in your life.

Hop to It

Tessa was born with a form of a cerebral palsy and was wheelchair bound. She made sure that you never noticed any defect with her big smile and her effervescent personality. Tessa's dad couldn't take the pressure of what he referred to as a broken child, and he was appalled that his wife refused to give her up. Before Tessa was even four months old he abandoned them. Tessa's mom, Sue, not only refused to give her up, she was Tessa's biggest cheerleader. She made sure that Tessa had the best care, medically and emotionally.

Tessa had frequent seizures and other ailments that made her disease severe. The doctors were surprised with every milestone she overcame. Sue was told that Tessa would likely pass away before her fifth birthday, but on her eighth birthday Sue took Tessa on a trip to a zoo that had an extensive amphibian display, where she was able to hold a variety of living and breathing amphibians. Her love of frogs began when she was gifted a stuffed frog, aptly named Froggy, on her first birthday. Froggy went everywhere with her and became a notorious icon to her nurses and doctors, getting "treated" with so-called ailments himself during her visits. Froggy was her legs, so to speak, and when Tessa was behaving especially difficultly, Sue would ask Froggy to help Tessa hop to it, whatever the *it* was in reference to at that moment. Tessa's mood would almost always fade at the irony of her mom asking a stuffed animal for help.

It was on the way home from her birthday trip when Tessa had the discussion of death with her mother. Sue never talked about the end—she was just trying to get her to the next step in life—but Tessa's health had been failing despite Sue pretending that it wasn't. Sue knew that Tessa knew.

"Mom, when I go to Heaven will you take care of Froggy?" Tessa innocently asked.

Sue bit her bottom lip to try and stop the tears from spilling over. Sue rarely cried, and she refused to do so on a celebratory occasion. "Tessa, I think Froggy should make the trip with you," Sue calmly answered.

"But I want him to take care of you. I know you'll be sad, and he could cheer you up!" Tessa said.

"Let's not talk about that right now, okay? How about some ice cream?" Sue asked in avoidance.

The discussion of Froggy was dropped and never picked back up. It wasn't until Tessa's funeral, one month later, that Sue had to wrestle with what to do. At the last minute, she tucked Froggy into the casket, placing him underneath Tessa's arm and kissing them both on their cheeks. "I think Froggy needs to make this trip with you," Sue whispered to Tessa.

Sue didn't have many friends, as there just wasn't any time for socializing, and most all of her family had passed away years before. She was grateful that several of Tessa's friends and their parents came to the funeral, along with several of Tessa's nurses throughout the years.

One of the nurses was a man named Frank, who had helped with Tessa's final transition. After her birthday, her seizures became worse, and she was hospitalized for twenty-three days before she passed. Tessa was kept mostly in a medical coma and then on life support, and Frank was the one who held Tessa's and Sue's hands when they removed the tubes and machines. It might not have seemed like a big deal to him, but Sue was grateful and made a mental note to send him a small gift after she had her life settled. *Life settled,* she sighed. She wasn't even sure what that might entail. Her biggest goal was keeping busy enough that she wouldn't have time to think. She wasn't sure she could survive if she had time to think.

The trip to the cemetery was a short one, just a couple blocks from the church. Sue watched the casket being lifted out of the hearse. She had saved for a year in order to give her daughter the pretty purple casket. She knew most people wouldn't understand that, but it was the last gift she would ever be able to give her little girl, and she wanted it to be perfect. And purple was Tessa's favorite color. As they lowered the casket into the ground, Sue wondered what she might have done in her life that would be deserving of this punishment, not just for herself but for that innocent little girl.

The small crowd disbursed with sad smiles and hugs, but Sue stayed, not wanting to leave. Not even sure where she would go. Home would be so quiet, she fretted. She had never left her daughter's side in all the years and all the hospital visits, and she wasn't sure how she was going to do it now. She watched the workmen cover the casket with dirt, pat it down, sprinkle grass seed over the freshly tilled ground, and then leave. Still, she sat there on the bench, simply staring. Knowing that she couldn't stay any longer, she walked over to the plot of land to say her final good-bye and noticed something on the ground that looked to be struggling. Kneeling down, she saw that it was a frog. Its legs were bound by a purple ribbon, more than likely from a balloon. Sue wasn't sure whether to laugh or to cry, but she knew she had to help the poor frog.

"Are you okay?"

Startled, Sue looked up from the frog to see Frank standing there.

"I'm so sorry. I didn't mean to frighten you," Frank said, shoving his hands into his coat pockets. "I waited in the parking lot to say good-bye, but you didn't come, and I got worried."

Sue nodded. Then she said, "Well, no, I guess I'm not okay, but I think this frog is worse than I am. Do you have a pocket knife by chance?" Sue held out the frog.

Frank slid a red Swiss Army knife out of his pocket and gently cut the ribbon while Sue untangled the frog's legs from it.

"There ya go," Sue said to the frog, as she set him on the ground atop her daughter's burial space. "Hop to it!"

The frog stretched its legs out, hopped for a bit, stopped, and simply sat, as if guarding Tessa's grave.

"It looks like Froggy came to life, huh?" Frank joked.

"Oh my goodness!" Sue gasped. "I know that's not really ture, but … do you believe in signs?"

"I do, and I think that little girl of yours gave you the first of many yet to come."

Sue smiled and looked down at the frog still sitting there. "I'm okay with that."

"Why don't we get you something to eat?" Frank suggested.

"I'd like that. Just no frog legs," Sue joked.

Sue had been worried she wouldn't have anything to do after Tessa's passing, but Frank became her constant companion. When he proposed to Sue, she knew that Tessa had helped from Heaven. The wedding was just months later; a simple affair at a local park with Frank's adult children and a few coworkers. As Sue walked down the gravel path to her new husband, she saw something jump in her path. She laughed in surprise when she discovered it was a frog.

"Did you bring a frog to our wedding?" Sue asked Frank after the ceremony.

Frank shook his head no. "I'm sure that was a gift from Tessa. And Froggy," he added.

Sue snuggled up to her new husband and thanked Tessa, and Froggy, for the constant signs and for her new husband.

We so often receive signs from our loved ones on the Other Side, and animals tend to be an easy one for those in Heaven to send us. Every animal has its own unique message associated to it. The frog is strongly linked to transformation and magic. Since frogs go through a transition from egg to tadpole and finally to their final form, the frog reminds us that we too can go through transformations that seem nearly impossible. So if you see a frog, it may be a message that you can accomplish anything and that you need, as Sue told Tessa so often, to hop to it.

Animals are all around us and offer easy ways for those on the Other Side to say they are around. It might be through that cardinal that chirps at your office window, the ladybug that lands on your hand, or even a fox that sits on your porch. We are surrounded by nature, and our loved ones often share a message through it, but we are so busy looking the other way that we miss it.

All Around

Signs are all around, and although you may be open to receiving them, it's so often chalked up to a weird coincidence or simply ignored. In need of a sign? Ask for one and then pay attention.

What Might Block Your Signs

- Sleep deprivation
- Sleeping aids
- Alcohol
- Drugs
- Stress

What Might Help You See Signs

- Healthy eating
- Water
- Exercise
- Routine sleeping patterns
- Consciously being alert

Chapter Four

Soul Scents

Skeptics claim that smells are a product of the mind. It can't be a spirit, they say, spirits are made up of energy, and scents are connected to matter not energy. There can be no denying it when others in the room smell the same scent, though.

Have you ever smelled something and there was nothing there to provide the scent? Some of the most common spirit scents seem to be cigar or cigarette smoke, perfume, mothballs, flowers, laundry detergent, and cooking specific items. *Clairalience* is the term used to describe the intuitive ability to smell scents from the spirit world.

Familiar scents can trigger memories and help make valid connections as to who is around. If all of a sudden you smell your grandma's spaghetti sauce cooking, it will often trigger a time when you were at her home, and then how you felt, how she made you feel, etc. It often awakens other intuitive connections as well.

A couple years ago I was in a car accident that tore my shoulder, and every so often I get horrific spasms that make even breathing excruciating. During one such episode, a phone call to my doctor resulted in him meeting me at his office after hours. I'm grateful to have a physician who may not understand what I do, but he is open minded about it. He also has studied alternative modalities such as Reiki, and that was one treatment he decided to try on me to help calm the pain.

As soon as I closed my eyes, I sensed the spirit of my mom walk in the room. Whenever I'm not feeling well or am hurting I will often sense her presence, but I've never had anyone else notice, until that evening that is.

My mom loved flowers, especially anything wild and untamed. The house I grew up in had lilac bushes all around, and when springtime came she would cut the bright purple blossoms and put them in vases in every room. It was the only thing she liked about our home.

Mom's sight was taken away from her when she was in her mid-forties. Doctors say that when a sense is dulled one or more of the other senses can become heightened, and she encountered the same phenomena. She had eagle ears and a sniffer like a search dog. Because of that she always wanted to be surrounded by delicious scents, beautiful music, and anything soft and comfortable. Even when she moved, the scent of lilacs was one of her favorites and she wore perfume that had a slight lilac scent to it.

Just as my physician began to do Reiki on me, the room filled with a beautiful lilac smell.

"Kristy, are you wearing lilac oil?" he asked me.

I laughed and replied that I wasn't. I, too, was smelling the fragrant lilacs and knew that it was simply my mom.

"Do you smell that?" he asked, confused and in awe.

"I do. It's actually from my mom. She's standing over in the corner."

"Oh, okay. Nice," he said, and continued to complete the healing.

A week or so later, I was back for another session. This time my grandfather decided to visit, and the room filled with a strong cigarette smoke.

"Do you smell that too?" my doctor asked, and I felt a bit of déjà vu.

Again I laughed, excited that his intuitive senses were so keen. "This time it's my grandpa," I shared.

"Could we possibly bring Mom back in? I liked the lilacs better." We both snickered.

Smell the Roses

Seen on popular paranormal shows such as *Ghost Adventures*, *Ghost Hunters Academy*, and *My Ghost Story*, the Ohio State Reformatory (or Mansfield Reformatory) in Mansfield, Ohio, has been noted as one of the top haunted locations in the world. It is utilized for many movie and music videos, most notoriously for the movie *Shawshank Redemption*. On a very hot day in August, I took a team of close to thirty to do an overnight to see if it lived up to the expectations.

The Ohio State Reformatory was built by Freemasons in 1886 and was designed to rehabilitate first-time offenders. The architecture was (and still is) spectacular, originally modeled to resemble a castle, and so it was thought that this would be a positive step for prison reform. Unfortunately, conditions rapidly deteriorated and this prison was left with a haunting legacy of abuse, inhumane torture, many murders, and secrets that are still contained within the walls. Civil Rights activists lobbied successfully to shut the prison down in 1990, as the prisoners resided with rats, bugs, bats, moldy and decaying food, and disease. Violence was an everyday occurrence, as was bloodshed. Five years later, in 1995, the Mansfield

Reformatory Preservation Society opened the prison for ghost tours.

One of the hot spots for paranormal activity is the warden's quarters. In the 1950s, the warden's wife, Helen Glattke, died under suspicious circumstances. According to reports, Helen was getting ready for church when she reached high on a closet shelf to pull down a jewelry box. A pistol, which was supposedly hidden inside a hat box, fell and discharged, killing her. Although her death was ruled accidental, it's Helen's spirit that seems to be one of the more active ones at the prison. There've been numerous reports that when she appears it is with the soft scent of rose oil.

Skeptical but interested, I led a small team to the warden's quarters. It's the most ornate and the cleanest of all the areas in the prison, so we all took a seat on the polished wood floors. We turned off the lights, including our flashlights and lanterns. The full moon's glow cast shadows along the walls, but a few minutes later clouds danced in front of our natural light and a fine mist hovered close to the closet doorway where the alleged accident happened. All at once, the smell of roses permeated the air.

It's human nature to question the senses, and someone asked if anyone else smelled the floral fragrance. Everyone in the group agreed they could smell it. One skeptical member went by the location and smelled the floor, thinking perhaps they were using a rose scented cleaner. Another member opened up the closet, thinking that someone had hidden an air freshener that would create the anomaly, but nothing was there. After attempting to debunk the smell, just as quickly as it came in to the room, it left. All at once the clouds scurried away from the moon and the room was once again filled with light.

Sometimes these are labeled phantom smells. I do believe that if you smell a scent without any source to attach it to, the phantom smell is likely a loved one on the Other Side visiting with a Heaven hello.

Stew This

Charlotte and Sean, a couple married for more than thirty years, sat with me for their session when Charlotte's mom, Ruth, came through in spirit. Ruth stood with a sour look on her face, as if I'd disturbed her. There's no conjuring when it comes to what I do. I honestly just call on anyone of the good and white light who wants to visit. They have the free will to come or not.

When I shared my observation, Charlotte's husband snickered. He explained that it was simply his mother-in-law's normal look, of which Ruth snarled in response, eliciting laughter from both Charlotte and Sean.

"Tell them I'm mad," Ruth shared. "I'm upset about the stew."

As if on cue, my office began to smell of the aroma of cooking stew meat, carrots, celery, potatoes, and spices. Nobody was in my building on that early Sunday morning, and we don't even have a kitchen, so the three of us looked at one another with surprise.

"Apparently your mom is upset about the stew. And I can even smell it. Heck, I can even taste it," I said.

The laughter continued between Charlotte and Sean. I could tell that it was an inside joke, so I asked them to share it.

"Mom was the cook in the family. She cooked for every holiday, birthday, and special occasion, but it was her famous stew that our family and friends loved. She refused to give out the recipe to even her kids. When we got older we would sneak in and try and figure it out, and she'd always run us out of the kitchen. The year she passed she wasn't doing well, and I think she knew it, so she called us all home for a family dinner of stew and homemade bread. When the stew was still on the stove, I took a taste, and it was horrible." Charlotte made a face. "I couldn't have her serve that, and I asked her what she put in it. Thinking that I was just trying to get her recipe, and just frustrated with the day, she took the whole pot of stew and threw it at the wall."

"That was her temper," Sean explained. "Apparently, she had spilled a whole salt shaker into the stew and thought she could cover it up somehow. We had to order pizza for dinner, and she was irate."

"She passed before she made another stew, but I sure miss Mom's cooking." Charlotte began to tear up.

I looked at Ruth, who looked sorrowful as well, and I felt bad for her. She just wanted that last supper to be special, and I think she had been more embarrassed than insulted.

"Tell her my secret ingredients are red wine vinegar and a dash of paprika," Ruth shared.

Charlotte quickly wrote it down and promised to let me know how it worked out. Just as quickly as we could smell the stew, the smell dissipated, as did Ruth.

It was a few months later when I received a photograph in my e-mail of a family dinner Charlotte had in her mom's memory. Everyone sat around the table enjoying Ruth's stew. "It still wasn't exactly like Mom's," Charlotte wrote. "I think she's still holding something back, but it was darn close."

The stew was the exact recipe, but it was missing Ruth.

Buttered Toast

Roy was broke and far from home when his mom called to tell him that his grandma would probably be passing in the next couple days. No money for a plane ticket or even gas for the car to get home, he sat at his kitchen table and cried. Then he suddenly smelled buttered rye toast and strong coffee.

"Those were the smells of my favorite mornings," he shared with me. "My family life was dysfunctional, and I'll keep it at that," he said. "When I was able to spend time with my grandparents, especially overnights, I was elated. It was the most stability I had and ever would have. My grandparents would get up with the chickens. Well, they didn't really have chickens," Roy grinned.

I laughed and looked over at his grandparents standing next to him, both in spirit and on the Other Side. They looked proud and happy.

"Oh, I loved lying in that small twin bed with the scratchy quilt on it, and hearing the quiet shuffling of my grandpa making coffee and my grandma fixing them buttered toast. I would grab a comic book—one that they would let me pick out every time they picked me up—get up, and sit at the small kitchen table. Grandpa would read the newspaper, I would read my comic, and Grandma would fix me breakfast. Every time I smell buttered toast I think of her. Is she mad at me, Kristy? I never got the chance to say good-bye."

"After you smelled the toast when your mom called, did your grandma pass soon after?"

Roy nodded. "Grandma didn't hang on. She must've died at the moment I smelled the toast."

"You got your good-bye then, Roy," I said quietly. "But she's not gone. She's right here, with your grandpa," I pointed over to where I could see them.

Roy grabbed a tissue and wiped his eyes. "I miss them. Bad."

"She says that she missed your grandpa and that she was so happy to join him. She knows that they were more like Mom and Dad than Grandma and Grandpa. She knows. Never think they are gone. And always know that when you smell that buttered toast, well, that's your Heaven hello."

I'm with You

Alex's grandpa wasn't allowed to smoke unless he was outside, and even then Grandma wasn't happy about his clothes smelling. Grandma worked hard outside the house and they didn't have an automatic washer, so it wasn't so easy to clean the clothes. Alex would sit on the back porch with Grandpa. He never said much, but she always felt loved and protected. It had been a long time since both her grandma and grandpa had passed, and it was during the hard times when she felt sentimental.

Alex had just signed the divorce papers when she was notified she had breast cancer and had to go for aggressive treatments. Feeling overwhelmed and alone, she sat in her car at the edge of a lake and contemplated leaving the world for good.

"I laid my head on the steering wheel and closed my eyes, ready to do something I now know is stupid. Immediately my car smelled of cherry pipe tobacco," Alex shared with the grief group that I was lecturing to.

"Nobody was in the car, and there wasn't any person or car anywhere to be seen. And then I heard my grandpa say in my head 'I'm with you,' and just as quickly as I smelled the tobacco, the smell dissipated."

The group nodded, as if remembering their own spiritual experience. Alex knew that it was her grandpa, and she picked up her cell phone and called for help.

Life is overwhelming and Heaven knows it. There comes a time when you must ask for assistance. Whether from those you love on the Other Side or from those around you. Your own pride can be a roadblock of energy and block the connection. Don't ever be afraid to ask for help.

Alex's grandpa thankfully got through. She not only found help, she got healthy and was cancer free just a year after her treatments.

Common Spirit Smells

- Cigar/cigarette smoke
- Pipe tobacco
- Perfume/aftershave
- Mothballs
- Menthol
- Chocolate
- Cooking food
- Flowers
- Laundry detergent
- Body soaps
- Baby powder
- Cleaning products
- Candles/incense
- Burning wood
- Coffee
- Gum

Chapter Five

Spirit Visitations

Spirit visitations are a wonderful way to connect with your loved ones on the Other Side. In the visit, they may talk to you and share a message or ask for you to share a message with someone else. Often they relay their afterlife peacefulness. You may find yourself in a garden, in a familiar location, or standing with them with a white light of love surrounding you.

Mass Visit

It was a warm winter evening when I had a visit that was a bit unusual, even for me. I dreamed that I was invited to go to a ticketed private event. I walked up a dirty path that led me to an old town church with peeling white paint. When I opened and walked through the large double front doors, a friend who passed away not long ago welcomed me, looked at my ticket, and pointed me into the packed church.

I walked the dusty wooden floors until I came to a larger room that had several wooden scrolled pews. Looking again at my ticket, I was in section N9, and as I looked around for it I recognized a

friend who'd passed away more than ten years before. As I continued to look around, I realized that every single person I ever knew
who had crossed over was there. My mom waved hello to me. My
grandpa winked at me. Another friend who passed in a car accident
smiled and nodded. Then the grandfather of my son's friend
came up, took my hand, and told me that I could sit with him in
the front row.

Before I could say anything, I woke up. It was so quick and I'd
have liked to dream longer. I woke up thinking of all the passings
I've had in my life and felt a deep sadness. After contemplating the
visit for a day, I realized that I was being selfish. Instead of being
upset and glum, the visit may very well have been teaching me to
see the blessings in all I had still with me in the physical. If anything, it was a wake-up call.

I'm Alive

Many people have visits where their loved ones on the Other Side
come to them to say they aren't dead, but very much alive. Because
of this news, they wake up frightened with all kinds of thoughts
running through their head. It's true, our loved ones aren't dead at
all. They live better than we live here in the physical plane, yet it's
often misunderstood as literal.

Not Just a Dream

Visits are one of the easiest ways that our loved ones on the Other
Side can communicate with us because we are meeting them half-
way. In our waking state we try to control and make sense of everything, but in our sleep state we let go of the control and remove
our roadblocks. Spirits need space in order to come through, and
during our sleep we offer that to them.

How Do You Receive a Visitation?

- Pay attention to what you might misinterpret as mere dreams. What may seem like a mere coincidence or seem weird, may actually be a visit.

- Work on your meditation in your waking state. Meditation helps to raise your vibration and puts you into an alpha state. It's that comfortable state of mind where you may still hear voices and noises going on around you, yet you are still in a sleep state. The more you work the meditation muscle, the easier it is to be in the alpha state during your sleep cycle. During an alpha state you may hear your name called and even have lucid dreams. You will be able to decipher your loved ones on the Other Side during meditation and your alpha state of sleep.

- Connect with your loved ones. Visualize what they look like, smell like, feel like, sound like, and so on. You might even want to look at a picture of them.

- Invite them in. Before you go to sleep, spend a moment and talk to your loved ones, inviting them to visit you in your dream state.

- Be patient. There is a long list of reasons why you aren't receiving a message, from deep grief to sleep medications.

- Give it time. I say to wait six months to a year before visiting a medium, as it takes time for your loved one to adjust to the Other Side, and you adjust to them not being here in the physical. It could take that amount of time as well for them to figure out how to come through with a visit and find their voice.

- Put a journal and pen by your bed. Jot down the date that you had the visit, as there may be significance (birth date, anniversary date, passing date, a passed surgery date, etc.), and then write down as much detail as you can remember. Once you get that visit, most details will be burned into your memory, but not everything is.

- Be patient again. Once you get that visit you will want another one and another one. It takes a lot of energy for the deceased to come through in any way, so be grateful and be patient, as it could be years before you receive another visit.

Visiting Hours

"It's the weirdest thing. I had a dream I was in my childhood home, sitting on the couch with my mom."

"That's beautiful," I bubbled. "Did it make you feel at peace?"

Jane smiled and nodded. "It's been six months since she passed, and I admit that I was feeling a bit sad not getting a sign. She hugged me so tight. Days afterward I could still feel her arms wrapped around me. What disturbed me, though, was she told me that she was very busy and it might be a bit before she visited again. Was that just a dream … or more?"

I looked over at Jane's mom, standing beside her in spirit. Her mom was a petite lady, maybe 4'7", and she said she'd been ill for years and was finally at peace.

"She's so excited that your dad is with her. She really missed him. She said that it's been about ten years since she's seen him."

Jane again nodded. "It's been ten years exactly."

"And she said that she missed her mom and dad, and her brother, too."

"Yep, Uncle Steve is there, too."

"It's not that she doesn't want to visit you. It's that she knows you are doing okay and, well, she needs a bit of a vacation. Kind of a honeymoon with your dad."

"I miss her too, though," Jane objected. "And really, what is there to do in Heaven?"

Not to be insensitive, but I couldn't help but laugh. I knew that Jane was grieving, and most people, including myself, grew up thinking that when we died we sang in the choir and played the cello. We only do that if we want to do that. Heaven is a busy place, where you get to pursue your passions and help guide people—both loved ones and ones who need love. Jane's mom had been gone less than a year, but to her mom it was still like yesterday. She was enjoying the company of her husband and her family. It was like she was resting or even vacationing. She also relayed to me that Jane's brother, Rod, was going through some serious medical treatments and that he needed her attention, too. I relayed the message.

Jane sighed heavily but expressed her understanding. "It's true, Rod hasn't been well, and we are all worried about him. I'm doing okay, except for missing her, and Rod does need her support. If she were here, she'd be with him. It makes sense."

"It doesn't mean she won't visit you, Jane. Or that she won't give you any signs, it's just that they may be more sporadic. So just be open to receiving them and not demanding them on your terms. Heaven has the upper hand," I revealed.

It wasn't long after the session that Jane contacted me with word that her brother, Rod, had passed away. It made sense why her mom was so busy. She told me that just a few days after her brother's passing she received a visit from her mom, dad, and Rod. They all sat around the dining room table and they just talked.

"The visit probably lasted all of a couple minutes, but it was so comforting to know that they were all together. I was grateful they were thinking enough of me to visit," Jane shared.

What Is a Visit?

A visitation is different from a dream. When you dream, you are re-creating subconscious thoughts and fears. Dreams are a way of processing feelings that are difficult to deal with in the conscious world. A visitation is when a deceased love one, a guide, and even angels communicate with you during your sleep, and it creates a deep and lasting impression.

Visitations feel very real and are extremely vivid, powerful, and something you can recall years later. While most dreams you often forget within minutes.

A visit also doesn't last very long from an earthly sense. It is often to the point, but it should leave you with the feeling of peace, healing, love, forgiveness, and sometimes reassurance.

You can typically tell the difference, although it is human nature to question it.

But Why Do I Feel Sad Afterward?

Many people describe feeling at peace but also a deep sadness for the following days and up to a week afterward. They may actually wake up with tears in their eyes after the visit. It isn't the intention of your loved one to make you feel sad, but it is an emotional event. Often there are suppressed feelings of grief, resentment, regret, guilt, and other emotions that still have to be released, no matter how long the loved one has been gone. The visit opens up those boxes of sentiments that were probably stored far away. It's a chance to really heal from the sadness.

A visit also conjures up feelings of missing, which is completely normal for us here in the physical world. We are such visual people that to get rid of the feeling of missing we often rid ourselves of memorabilia and pictures—anything visual that reminds us of that person. We do this after a breakup, but we also do this after a death. When we have the visit, we have a visual reminder of the loss. Brazilians call that missing *saudade*, which is a longing or melancholy feeling, especially when thinking of someone who has passed away.

Was It Just a Dream?

A man came up to me after a lecture on dreams and visits that I gave at a local library and introduced himself as Brad.

"So, Kristy, my dad passed two years ago, and, probably because I was coming here, I dreamed that I was at my dad's funeral. As I stepped toward his casket, he sat up and started screaming at me about crazy random things. If that was a visit, it sure wasn't peaceful. I'm still wondering what I did that he might be mad at me for."

It was a common dream and a common debate that many wrestled with, but it was just a dream.

"What are you feeling guilty about, Brad? What is it, with regard to your dad's passing, that you feel you should've done differently and you blame yourself for?"

Brad's face turned red, and he began to tear up. "On the day my dad died, I left early to go visit him in the hospital, but instead I swung by the golf course to release some stress. He died before I got there. If I hadn't gone golfing I would've been able to say my goodbye."

"That's it," I confirmed. "See, it isn't that your dad is mad at you, it's that you are mad at yourself. Your dream was transferring that guilt and anger to your dad since it was about him. Make sense?"

"So Dad's not mad at me?"

I shook my head no. "He's not mad, and he's at peace. Now it's time for you to find peace too, so you can have a real visit."

Brad graciously thanked me.

I've had numerous people have similar casket or funeral dreams where their loved one expressed their dissatisfactions and the majority of them were just a dream.

Chapter Six

Spirit Lights

Spirits show themselves to us all of the time, and we are often so busy with this or that and discount it as strange or weird and nothing more. One of the more interesting ways that spirit can show themselves to us is through what some call spirit lights. Others have described it as spirit glitter, orbs, bubbles, or sparkles.

It was a Halloween evening and I was conducting an event when a lady raised her hand. Shyly she asked me what the sparkles were all around me. "It looks like someone sprinkled gold glitter down on you," she described.

Another lady in the audience gasped. "I saw it too and thought maybe something was wrong with my eyes." A half a dozen others agreed and shared they too had seen flashes of light or sparkles.

It was spirit, I explained. It was simply spirit energy and they can be seen in daylight or nighttime.

Kids often see the phenomena. Babies often grasp in the air and giggle, although you may not see anything, they are catching sight of spirit energy.

Although not a fan of orbs in photos, I've witnessed some amazing orbs with the naked eye that could only be explained as spirits.

Gettysburg

One autumn, my husband and I went to Gettysburg, Pennsylvania, for an anniversary trip. We decided to take a tour of the battlefield before calling it a night. The battlefield at the time closed at ten o'clock, but it was only eight and inky black. We were instructed by a friend to drive into the park, shut the car off, and simply listen to the echoes of history. Listen to the battle cries and the cannon fires. The battlefield comes alive at night, he told us.

So we parked on the side of the road and turned the car off as instructed. It was only a moment after that we saw a bright white light coming up behind us. We thought at first that it was a motorcycle or a three-wheeler, but as it neared, we saw that it was a floating orb. It came up around the back of our car to the driver side window and briefly stopped before continuing on into the fields. Not a tiny dusty particle size, but the size of two beach balls together. Chuck and I looked at one another, aghast, and then we began to hear the sounds of war. A bit spooked, Chuck started the car and drove to another part of the grounds where there was an observation tower.

Chuck stopped at the tower. "Want to climb it with me?" he asked.

I shook my head and laughed. Not only did I dislike heights, I really disliked heights in the dark. Chuck was bound and determined, and with a camera and cell phone as his only light, he made the climb. Minutes later, I could hear footsteps clang on the metal steps as he ran back down. Breathless, he explained that he felt someone up there with him, but even more bewildered, he said he saw lights in the field and soldiers standing, kneeling, and lying down.

"Did you take photos?" I asked, grabbing the camera from him and hitting the menu button to scroll through.

He had, and on the photos were green illuminations in the form of soldiers. They weren't reenactors either, as I tried to debunk our experience. We were privy to the experience of spirit lights.

Candid Camera

"What do you think of this, Kristy?" An elderly women came up to me after an event and handed me a photograph of several people sitting around a table with food. "This was taken at my husband's wake and look, right there," she said pointing to an obvious finger that had slipped on the lens. "Do you see it? Do you think it was Walt saying he was okay?"

I'm often asked to decipher anomalies in photos and say whether it is a spirit or not. Whether a light strand, a stray hair, a thumbprint, or various orbs, many obsess over photographs or do something called matrixing or *Pareidolia*. Matrixing is when your mind takes an image and makes it into something familiar, even if that image isn't truly there. So the orb that looks just like Uncle Jim's face, mustache and all, is more than likely just an orb and came from your dog's dander. Or if you've ever looked at the clouds in the sky and saw an elephant riding a skateboard and your spouse saw an ostrich with a lion on its back—that's matrixing.

Reflections from glasses, windows, and doors can also create the perceived image that an ethereal being is visiting. I've seen some interesting photographs taken outside that look to be a person standing there, when really it is just the way the tree and branches are formed.

"I do see that. I'm not sure if it is Walt, but I'm sure that he's fine. He hopes that you know he's at peace. He probably was drooling over all that yummy food I see there in that photograph."

The lady smiled, put the photograph back in her purse, and turned to look at her daughter. "See, I told you it was Dad." She then walked away.

I told a partial white lie. I've been handed photographs with people in front of their Christmas trees or another light source and they were sure it was a deceased loved one because of the oddities that showed up from the reflections of the lights. I admit that I often nod and smile rather than deflate the peace the photograph gives them.

We are made up of energy, and although our physical body no longer exists, our energy does. Energy can indeed show up in photographs; I'm not denying that. For as many iffy photographs I've been shown, I've also been shown some interesting ones that offer no explanation other than the possibility of spirit. They are depicted with shadows, strange strands of lights, and even full-blown apparitions. Although with all of the applications on the smart phones, there are many fraudulent photos, too. There is a lot to consider before recognizing the photograph as possible spirit, and for me it is the validity and reputation of the person.

Family Reunion

"I think you need to see this, Kristy," my friend Bretta said, handing me a photograph. "I took this at the family reunion this weekend. I saw it on the camera screen afterward and printed it. What do you see?"

I didn't have to cock my head to one side or the other to see what she was referring too, which was a plus in itself. There, in the corner of the picture, standing next to Bretta's son, was an image of a man who looked as if it formed from smoke. The features were prominent, as were the clothing.

"Bretta, that's your dad! Look at the nose and the mouth. Look at the beige shirt he wore all of the time, he's wearing it right here!" I exclaimed. Even though I trusted Bretta, I still have a tendency to try and debunk. "Was there another relative there who looks like your dad? Or a mirror with a picture of your dad? Or anything that could've conjured up a reflection of your dad?"

"Nope, not at all. What do you think it means?"

It obviously was a display of love. The image of Bretta's dad was standing next to his grandson, looking down on him. "He's watching over Justice, Bret. He said he would do that before he passed. He was a man of his word, and right here, he's showing you that." I pointed to the photo and handed it back to her.

It was beautiful.

I had another client show me a photograph she took of her husband as he was passing away in the hospital. All the family members were standing around the bed, and in the picture were tiny white lights floating above her husband's head. Although that was impressive, it was what was in the corner that made me gasp. In the corner of the hospital room was an image of a bright light and what looked to be angel wings coming from it. The picture was in focus and clear, yet there it was.

Yet another photograph a client showed me was taken at her grandparents' home years after both her grandpa and grandma passed away. Nobody was home, but there was an image of a lady sitting on a bench in the garden. It was wispy looking, but the detail was there down to the dress her grandma used to wear.

There will always be disbelievers and skeptics, and, as I said, by all means attempt to debunk it. But sometimes there is no explanation and that too has to be accepted.

Nana

It was a warm October Friday afternoon when my son, daughter, husband, sister, and niece ventured to a friend's farm to get some apple cider and cinnamon donuts. It's a popular tradition in Michigan, and our friend's farm was one of our favorite spots. Not only did they have yummy food, they also had animals and a haunted house. After picking out our treats, our friend asked if the kids wanted to go through the haunted house.

"The monsters are just starting to warm up for the evening rush," she said. "Here are tickets. Go have fun."

Even though I deal with the paranormal and the spirit world, I've never been a fan of jump-out-at-you entertainment. The last time I went to a Halloweenlike haunted house, a guy in my group had to carry me out because I was crying so hard. I admit I'm a sissy. Give me a poltergeist over a man dressed as a knife-wielding clown any day. My daughter and niece decided that they wanted to go through, and my friend asked if we wanted to watch them on their cameras, so we agreed. The girls rushed off to begin their haunted adventure.

Grabbing a chair in front of their monitors, we saw that each room had a camera in it. We watched the girls carefully step into the first room. Immediately, a large bright orb appeared in back of the girls.

"What is that?" Chuck asked, pointing to the orb.

We all looked at the screen, and then at one another, and then back to the screen.

"I think that's my mom," I whispered. "She never liked anything scary either. She's probably protecting them."

The group watched as the girls went from room to room, with a monster jumping out of hidden walls or chasing them in each room. All the while, the bright white orb swayed and moved, making sure to be between them and the monster. We were all awestruck as we watched this spirit light maneuver its way with the girls.

"I've never seen this before," my friend commented. "And I watch these all night long!"

Just as the girls stepped out of the haunted house, the orb disappeared. We decided to watch for a while longer as others went through, but no orb appeared. Feeling confident that we debunked there being a problem with the cameras, we took it as a heavenly sign.

Some have reported a pulsing orb and heard voices in their head, as if the spirit was communicating with them. This happened to a young teacher named Ida, who was a substitute for Kay, the seasoned instructor who was out on long-term disability. Unfortunately, Kay passed away, and Ida was offered the job of teaching second grade. Ida decided to decorate the classroom one evening when she noticed a bright light. "I felt like I was being watched," she explained. "It pulsed several times and then simply disappeared. What was weird was that I swear I heard Kay's voice in my head, telling me to take care of her kids. She named one in particular. The next week I noticed bruises on the child I heard Kay tell me to watch over. Come to find out he had a broken leg from his mother's boyfriend throwing him down the stairs. I'm not sure I would've noticed if it wasn't for that voice."

We All Have the Ability to Experience Spirit Lights

Shut all of the lights off in your bedroom and lay down. Ask your guides and loved ones to join you by showing you lights. Keep your eyes open and be careful to not rub them, just allow yourself to get used to the darkness. Notice any swaying in the energy. You might see energy moving around. Eventually the dark energy will turn to light. It may take some time before you see it.

Many times our loved ones visit us while we sleep, and you may wake up with a bright light around you, as if headlights are shining in your bedroom window, and then it disappears just as fast. This too is spirit light.

NOTE: If you are experiencing floaters or frequent orbs or irregularities, I suggest getting your eyes checked just to be on the safe side.

Sunshine on Your Shoulders

She was going to be a princess when she grew up. Or an astronaut. Or a ballerina dancer. It just depended on the day you asked her. She was five years old with the sass of a fifteen-year-old, the wisdom of a hundred-and-fifteen-year-old, and a smile that could make the crankiest person happy again. It was apropos that she was named Sunny.

It was just a few weeks after Sunny began kindergarten when her mom, Olivia, noticed that Sunny was more tired than normal. "It's probably just the schedule change," Lou, her husband, discounted. But there was something else, call it a mother's intuition. It was a gray Saturday morning when Sunny woke up vomiting and with a severe headache. It was the longest ride that Olivia had ever taken, holding her sick little girl in the back seat while Lou quickly drove them the few miles to the emergency room.

As slow as the drive seemed, the rest was a blur of doctors, tests, more doctors, and more tests. It didn't take long for the diagnosis that Sunny had an inoperable and terminal brain tumor.

"How long does she have?" Lou asked the doctors.

"Not long," was the reply. They promised to make her comfortable until it was her time, and they arranged for a team of medical professionals to assist them with Sunny's last days.

Although Sunny was in pain, she kept her sunny disposition and tried to make her parents giggle as much as she could. They tried to mask their sadness, but they knew they weren't fooling anyone, especially Sunny.

"I'm just going to make her as happy as I can," Olivia cried, talking to her best friend. "If she wants a milk shake, I will run out and get a milk shake. If she wants a baby doll, I will go get that. I don't care what it is, I will get it for her."

The next morning, Olivia went to check on Sunny for the hundredth time. It had been three weeks since the diagnosis and they had moved her home.

"Mommy, can you sit with me?" Sunny said, patting the bed next to her.

Olivia stopped fussing and sat down, stroking her only child's corn-colored hair.

"Mommy, I want you to be happy when I go. You always said I was your sunshine. I will still be your sunshine. I promise!"

Olivia couldn't help but sniffle and wrap Sunny in her arms, holding tight and hoping to never have to let go. But that night Sunny slipped into unconsciousness and was shuffled off to the hospital, where she passed away the next day. Olivia, Lou, and their parents sang through their sobs "You are My Sunshine" at Sunny's bedside. Just as a caseworker and doctor came in to speak with them, a ray of sunshine peeked through the hospital blinds and lit up Olivia.

"Look." Lou pointed. "You have sunshine on your shoulder, Liv."

Olivia tried to smile, but she dismissed it as a sign. *It's too early for a sign,* she thought.

"I know this is a tough time," the caseworker began, "but we have a little girl, a couple years older than Sunny who was born with cystic fibrosis and will die if she doesn't have a lung transplant soon. Sunny and her are the same blood type and well ..."

"Have you thought of donating Sunny's organs?" the doctor finished. "I'd love to give you time to think about it, but time is something we just don't have."

Olivia looked at Lou, and they both nodded in agreement. They couldn't live feeling responsible that another little girl might die and they could have helped. They knew Sunny would want it, too.

When they took Sunny's body away, Olivia couldn't help but have a breakdown. Lou was never an affectionate husband, but he was a loving one and he loved Sunny too. Lou took Olivia in his arms and held her as she punched and scratched, yelled and screamed. None of it was fair, and Lou felt disappointed that he couldn't do anything to bring Sunny back or make his wife stop hurting.

The next day they received a phone call from Sunny's doctor. "Again, I'm so sorry for your loss. I did, though, want you to know Sunny didn't just save one little girl, she saved four people yesterday. They are all doing wonderfully."

They say that the tiniest of coffins is the heaviest. They put their baby girl to rest on a sunny day less than a month after her diagnosis. Her grave sat in a field of cornflowers and tall pines. It didn't bring Sunny back, but Olivia and Lou weren't regretful about their decision.

Two years after Sunny's passing, Lou and Olivia met at the hospital where they had said their final good-bye to Sunny to say hello to one of the recipients of her donations. It was an emotional welcoming, and the tears especially flowed when the doctor handed Olivia the stethoscope to hear Sunny's heart beating strongly in a young boy named Landon.

Just as it did after Sunny passed, a bright ray of sunshine streamed through the blinds, blinding Landon and Olivia. "Look," Lou whispered. "It's Sunny."

Olivia smiled. It was a constant occurrence, especially in photos. It seemed every photograph of them had a stream of light shining on them. The photo could be inside or out, it didn't matter, there was always a light.

"Did Sunny love peanut butter and raspberry jam sandwiches?" Landon asked.

Olivia looked at him puzzled. "Yes, exactly. But not grape jelly. She hated grape jelly."

Landon's mom gasped. "Landon used to love everything grape and now he refuses to eat it. And I heard you talking about the stream of light, look…" She pulled out several photographs taken of Landon when he was in the hospital recovering from the transplant. Each one showed a stream of light shining on him. "It looks like Sunny was watching out for him, too."

Sunny would always be their sunshine, and now it seemed she was looking down on the ones she helped save.

Chapter Seven

The Delay

A soul doesn't have to cross immediately. Choosing when to cross is part of our free will. That doesn't mean that they stay earthbound or stuck either, but instead delayed. A delay can happen due to concern for their loved ones still here, and they can even help in urgent situations. They often appear in the physical, just the way they did when they passed, down to the jewelry they were wearing, and assist in emergency situations.

The Waiting Room

Dalia and her mom, June, were out on a Saturday afternoon looking for yard and estate sales. It had always been a beautiful bonding time for the both of them when Dalia was younger, but unfortunately there just never seemed to be enough time in the day, or the months, or the years. Dalia had her own kids and knew that her mom wasn't getting any younger. She was excited to once again share the mother-daughter experience.

It wasn't even noon and they had already visited five locations and found some small treasures. They decided to get a bite and venture out again. It was a late spring day, but the temperatures were warm and the sun was shining. Just a few feet before their lunch destination a car crossed the median and ran head on into Dalia's car, pushing it into a tree. June felt blood trickle down her cheek and opened her eyes.

"Mom! Mom!" Dalia cried. "You have to get your seat belt off now and crawl out."

June thought her arm must've been broke, as she couldn't seem to move to release the buckle.

"Here, let me help," Dalia leaned in and unbuckled June's seat belt. "Hold on, Mom. I'll get out and try and open your door."

Dalia exited her door, ran over to June, and was able to open the door just enough for June to wiggle out.

The emergency sirens were close. Just as June took a few steps away from the car, a paramedic pulled her into the back of his truck to evaluate her. A policemen ran to the car and then back over to June.

"Where's Dalia? She was right here. Dalia! Dalia!" June called out.

The paramedic and police officer looked at one another before the officer gently told June that her daughter didn't make it. June ran over to the car to see Dalia slouched across the steering wheel, seat belt on, and dead.

"Not only did I see her," June told me one afternoon at her appointment, "but the restaurant owner who called 911 also saw her run over to me. It made absolutely no sense at the time."

I nodded sympathetically.

"It took me a long time to realize she really did die, at least that her body did. The police gave me the photos, even though they didn't want to. I would stare at the crushed metal for hours, trying to wrap my head around it all."

"Do you still feel her around you?" I asked.

"I do," June confirmed. "She had a spirit that would help anyone, anytime, and anyway."

"She still does," I said. "That won't ever go away. Our personality isn't attached to our physical body; it is part of our spirit and soul."

June was a witness to unconditional love.

I could feel Dalia's spirit on the Other Side, and she came through for June with her grandparents and the family dog, Mutt. Dalia was okay, but she was sad that her passing happened the way that it did.

"Mom was with me at birth, and sadly at re-birth," Dalia said. "Tell her that I'm good, though. I'm good."

I'm sure it fell on deaf ears, as June would always grieve her daughter's passing on a random Saturday afternoon, but I passed the message along.

"Tell Mom at least that vase I bought didn't break in the car crash."

June laughed. "That sounds just like her to be more worried about a fifty-cent yard sale find."

You can't kill the spirit and soul, which is made up of our personality, beliefs, love, and even sense of humor.

Saving Grace

It was a Saturday morning when Officer Larry Lightner and his partner Elwin Jacobson sat down across from me, both looking nervous.

"We don't really know how this works," Elwin said, looking around my office.

"Yeah, no rooster feathers or shrunken heads here," I joked.

Larry laughed and excused his partner. "He's a bit spooked." He smiled.

Elwin darted his partner a dirty look. "Well, okay, me too," Larry admitted.

I nodded. I understood. I could still remember how nervous I was at my first reading.

"What I typically do is call on your guides, my guides, and any loved ones who want to pass along a message. I then give it to you. Feel free to stop me if you are confused or have questions. But my problem is that I don't think you are here for a connection, are you?" I explained to them both.

Larry and Elwin both shook their heads in unison.

"We saw, gosh, I don't even know how to say this without sounding absolutely nuts," Elwin sighed.

"We were called to an accident. A car had plunged off a ravine, rolled, and landed upside down in the river," Larry started, looking down at his hands. "Elwin and I were the first at the scene. A lady wearing a jean coat and khakis came running over to us, telling us her baby was in the car. We didn't wait for more help; we both ran down the ravine to the car."

"I still don't know how we did it, but the back window was cracked and water was filing up the car. I reached in and grabbed a baby out of her car seat. She had to be no older than six months old," Larry continued. "I looked around the car for any other victims and there in the driver seat was a lady ..."

"Wearing a blue jean jacket and khakis. And dead," I finished.

The officers both nodded.

"We both saw her. Others even saw her, but how?"

"Energy is very strong and you can't kill it, it just transfers. I'm sure that the mom's physical body had died, but her soul and her spirit were still strong, and still are. She knew that she needed to save her baby. Just like during a stressful situation when you get an adrenaline rush, the spirit can have a similar effect and she used it to contact you both. It was her deep motherly love that knew she had to find someone to save Grace."

"How did you know the baby's name?" Elwin asked curiously.

I answered with just a smile when Larry answered, "Umm, she's a medium!"

Baby Grace did survive her ordeal. I'm sure that her mom was thankful to the officers for risking their lives to save her precious cargo.

Overcrowded

It's been found that when a large number of people pass at the same time some miss the bus, if you will, to Heaven. They stay earthbound, confused and wandering.

In 2016, cab drivers in Japan divulged that they've been having ghost passengers. According to a story on MSN.com, "At least seven taxi drivers in Ishinomaki, northeast Japan, have reported experiencing a 'phantom fare' in the wake of the devastating 2011 tsunami and earthquake. In each instance, the story is similar. A taxi driver in northeast Japan picks up a passenger in an area devastated by the 2011 earthquake and tsunami. He starts the meter and asks for the destination, to which the customer gives a strange response. Either then, or sometime later, the driver turns around to address the man or woman—but the passenger has vanished. This is because, it is claimed, it was a 'ghost passenger' who was, in fact, killed in the disaster five years ago."

Stories just like that one have been reported in almost every disaster, in every location, including the Oklahoma bombing and September eleventh.

Harvey owned a small café near the World Trade Center and saw the devastation firsthand. The week after, when life began to get somewhat normal again, Harvey reopened his shop. Within the hour, he was having frantic customers rush in asking to use his telephone, only for them to vanish in front of him. "I thought I was losing my mind," he told me, "but when my wife came in and the same thing happened with her, and then my neighbors shared similar experiences, I realized that it was lost souls. Instead of handing them the phone, I told them that they needed to go into the light and find peace. I also blessed my building."

Once in a great while, he still receives a visit from a confused spirit, but they are few and far between now.

When we experience something scary or tragic, typically our first thoughts are to call or speak to our loved ones. The same holds true for those who pass away.

Chapter Eight

The Transition

The deathbed vision phenomena can only be explained as supernatural, and most things supernatural can't be explained. Deathbed visions have a beautiful purpose, though, offering comfort and a sense of familiarity to the dying. Family members and caregivers who understand the same can find peace that their loved ones are being joined by family and friends who will help with the transition to the Other Side. Their soul and spirit are simply preparing for their journey as they are met by loved ones and even angels. It is far more uncommon for someone not to have a deathbed experience than to have them.

Just as the family gathers at the hospital to celebrate the birth of a new baby, loved ones gather to celebrate the re-birth to the Other Side.

I Can't Remember

My children's great-grandmother on their father's side fought a terrible battle with Alzheimer's disease. She had grown up in France before meeting her military husband, who brought her to the

United States. When the disease took hold, she missed her home country. She ached for the comfort of the familiar, and even though it had been decades since she'd been back to her France, the memory of it all was front and center. She couldn't remember that she had children, but she could remember her favorite crepes and what the streets looked like. She would often run away, hoping to find it again, only to be caught by the police and brought back to a home she had lived in for more than fifty years but couldn't remember. She accused everyone of stealing from her, especially food, despite the refrigerator being full. Her calm and lovely personality changed to angry and feisty. The only thing that calmed her was when she received visits from her husband and other family members, all of whom had passed away years before. She would share their in-depth conversations and conjure up stories from the past, as if they were truly sitting right there with her. Or were they?

Hallucinations are common with those diagnosed with Alzheimer's disease and other dementias, or so says modern medicine. However, the disease forces their brain to regress to an open-minded state, removing the blocks that society seems to put in place. It isn't unusual for those suffering with Alzheimer's or dementia to have a direct link to the Other Side and see and converse with their loved ones who have passed away. Just because we can't see them, doesn't mean they aren't there.

With the loss of memory, skills, and independence, frustration is common, but sometimes the frustration also comes from their experiences with the Other Side and not understanding that others are unable to see what they see. Oftentimes those with a neurological disease forget those living but remember those who have crossed over. They may see their loved ones who are on the Other Side; they may see angels, spirits, light anomalies, and shadows. It is the way that the Other Side actually helps them cope with the frustration and stress. Just as young kids often see spirits and have paranormal occurrences, so do those near death. The veil to the Other Side is thin to those who were recently birthed and those about to be reborn in the spirit. As a medium, I often see or sense the energy of those with dementias or Alzheimer's on the Other Side in lieu of on Earth. It's as if they walk between the two worlds. It is the same for those who are nearing their transition.

Calling Mom Home

"Mom, Dad's been gone for years, how many times do I have to tell you that?" Anne snapped at her mom.

Anne felt bad for being abrupt, but the last couple weeks her mom had tall tales of her dad visiting her and then would be distraught and confused as to why he wasn't by her side. The problem was that her dad had passed away from lung cancer five years before. It was soon after that her mom was diagnosed with Alzheimer's, a disease Anne wouldn't wish on her worst enemy or their family.

"I know that my mind isn't always together," Anne's mom said, "but Dad was just here, and he said he was coming back tonight to take me on a vacation. Oh, I love trips, Laura. I wonder where we are going!"

Anne simply shook her head. There was no use correcting that Mom called her by her sister's name or arguing over the fact that her dad was gone or that there wouldn't be a trip at all. She was grateful, however, that the disease hadn't made her mom an angry and mean person. If anything, she was like an innocent child who didn't have a care in the world.

Anne was also thankful for wonderful nurses who cared for her mom in a wonderful facility. As much as she would've taken her mom in to her home, her own life was riddled with sorrow and confusion. She felt cheated that she wasn't able to grieve her own dad's passing before going into caretaker mode for her mom. It was soon after the funeral that her husband filed for divorce and her only child graduated from high school and moved to college. Her siblings felt that their mom would be best in the facility that she was in now, worried that if she stayed with Anne, Anne would never move on with her life. Anne came every single day, though, to sit with her mom, but the last week had been the hardest yet. She was missing her dad and missing her mom, even with Mom right in front of her, and she was confused about her own life path.

"Kristy, she's driving me nuts," Anne confessed to me in her session. "She tells very detailed stories about my dad being there. Just this morning she said that he was going to take her on a trip. A trip, of all things!" she laughed.

"Don't be upset with me ...," I began.

Anne looked at me, confused.

"Your dad is standing next to you. He's so handsome. He sort of looks like Clint Eastwood, with a quiet but determined energy." I smiled. "He's a lot like you. He says he is coming for Mom, and as much as they have no time in the afterlife, it could be soon. Real soon," I cautioned.

I was always very careful with expiration dates, as I didn't feel that it was my job to be the Grim Reaper. I did, and still do, believe in free will and free choice, and that nothing is quite set in stone. Just as pregnant moms are given a due date, yet it could be before or after that date, I believe the death date can change as well.

"Oh, Kristy, except for the memory loss, she's healthier than I am! The doctor even said that to me yesterday."

"Dad just wants you to be prepared for the unexpected."

"That sounds like my dad," Anne sighed. "Before his passing ..."

"He had every legal and estate issue taken care of and had even written all of you good-bye notes," I interrupted.

"Yes! How did you …?"

Anne grinned when I pointed over to where her dad was standing.

"Anne, Dad said that when Mom crosses, he wants you to move on, too. As much as you don't feel the need to go on a date, there's going to be a man that both your parents will send to you. You will know who that is, and you already know him."

She squinted at me and shook her head. "Never. Ever. Ever." She made sure to emphasize each word.

"Send me a wedding invite, okay?"

She laughed at me and we continued on with her session.

The next afternoon, I received an e-mail from Anne.

Kristy,

Last night I had the oddest dream. My dad came to me and handed me his wedding ring and told me that it was my time. I woke up to my phone ringing and it was a call that I wasn't prepared for—Mom passed away in her sleep. I know that you and him tried to prepare me, and I'm sorry I doubted you both. I guess I will send you an invite to my wedding when it happens.

Sincerely,
Anne

Two years later, I received the wedding invitation. Anne's dad said it was a man that she knew, and wouldn't you know that it was. Anne decided to attend her high school reunion, where she met up with her old next door neighbor and classmate. They got to talking and, well, the wedding was a beautiful summer event under the stars in northern Michigan where they exchanged rings. Anne gave

Rick her dad's wedding band and Rick had the jeweler create a ring just for Anne out of her mom's wedding ring and his mom's wedding ring, who was also on the Other Side.

A Foot in Two Worlds

As death draws near, many experience visits or visions from their friends and relatives who have crossed over. As the physical body begins to pass, those visits often become more frequent. They just don't feel real, they are real. These visions or visits have varying time lines from months before a passing to hours, but they all have a constant in that they bring amazing peace to those with a foot in both worlds. It is the living who are often confused.

The bond of love doesn't leave with death.

Deathbed Vision Tips

- Don't tell the dying that what they are seeing, hearing, or experiencing isn't there. Instead, ask your loved one for more information on what they are experiencing, such as, "Mom, what is Dad telling you?" Or say, "Tell me more. What is it that you see?"

- Offer them comfort in their experiences. "I'm so happy Dad is with you, Mom."

- Don't ever underestimate what your dying loved one is seeing or going through. Keep an open mind. Just as every birth is unique, every death is unique as well.

Afterlife Vows

I had met with Joel, whose wife had been fighting to live for several years after being diagnosed with leukemia. Everyone knew she didn't have long. As she lay in her bed at home, still fighting, he asked if I'd possibly Skype with her, and we agreed on a mutual day and time. For almost an hour, Angie and I talked about Heaven, death, and the afterlife. She shared seeing loved ones in spirit and being surprised that she could. She shared her fears of what would happen to her husband and her children.

"It's not my fear of stepping over the threshold into the afterlife," she explained, "it's that Joel and the kids won't be able to get along without me." Angie hesitated a moment and added, "And then I'm afraid that they will get along just fine without me."

Joel broke down crying after hearing Angie's reason for holding on for so long.

"Pick a day and time you will talk from the Other Side and will send a sign," I suggested.

"How's Wednesdays at noon?" Angie said to Joel, who nodded in agreement. "I'd like to send you a butterfly. Not just any butterfly but a bright yellow butterfly that will land on you. There won't be any debating that it's me."

Angie and Joel sealed their afterlife vow with a kiss.

The next week, Joel called to tell me that Angie passed peacefully the afternoon of our visit—it was Wednesday at noon. He said she smiled like she had a secret and took her last breath.

"I was at the cemetery saying my good-bye and guess what landed on me," Joel laughed.

Angie sent her bright yellow butterfly to sit on Joel's shoulder for several minutes. Then it flew away. Joel continues to set his alarm for Wednesdays at noon to call his wife on the Other Side for their date. He says that sometimes he hears her voice in his head, and other times it feels as if he's leaving a voice mail for her, but he knows she's around.

The Mystery of Miceli

The family gathered around Salvador's hospital bed to say their good-bye. Hospice said it was a matter of days, if not hours, before he would pass away. Sal had been in a prolonged state of delirium for several days and was calling out greetings to people, all of whom had been deceased for years. At one point, he sat up in the bed and smiled a huge smile, looking over into the corner of the room and addressing someone he called Miceli. Sal came from a large Sicilian family and although there were many relatives, all of those Sal mentioned could be claimed. Nobody knew who Miceli was.

"It's probably the medicine," Pauline, his wife, tried explaining to the family.

But Sal continued to call out greetings to people. The room seemed to get busier and busier with both living and passed relatives.

"I think he's really seeing them," Vito, Sal's nephew, said after a new group of invisible people showed up, all once again welcomed by Sal.

"I can't believe you finally met Miceli, Mom," Sal exclaimed, his hands wildly flailing in excitement. "I knew you'd love him like I did."

Everyone just stared at Sal and then looked at one another for an explanation, shrugging in confusion as to who the mystery man was that Sal's mom finally got to meet on the Other Side.

That evening, just before the clock struck eleven, Sal sat up in his bed again, grabbed Pauline's hand, and pressed it to his lips. "I will always love you, my darling. I will always be with you. I now know that to be the truth after seeing Miceli." He rested his head back down on the pillow and took his last breath.

With the busyness of the funeral, Pauline and Sal's family forgot all about Sal's bedside vision, that was until a week after Pauline was going through the pile of cards she'd received. Inside one of the cards was a letter.

Dear Pauline,

I heard of Sal's passing and felt the need to write to you. You don't know me, and Sal probably never mentioned me or my husband before. My husband, Miceli, and your husband were platoon buddies in the Army when they were both just 18 years old. No, they were more than buddies, they were more like brothers. Miceli and I got married when I was just 19 years old and soon after I became pregnant and had a baby boy that I named Salvatore after your husband. You see, your husband saved my husband's life in the war, and if it weren't for him I wouldn't have been able to enjoy my husband for as long as I got him. The post-traumatic stress was just too much and it took a toll and not long after their term ended, Miceli committed suicide. Sal came to me and said that he wished me well, but he was so angry with Miceli, and he was sorry, but he couldn't keep in contact with me afterward. He didn't feel that it was healthy for either of us. What Sal didn't know was that I had been writing to his mom during their deployment. My own mom had passed away and my worries were her worries and we bonded. Again, it was like Miceli and Sal were like brothers, only Sal's mom passed a day before Miceli took his life and I lost everyone, except my sweet son. I saw Sal's obituary in the paper and wanted to extend my friendship to you. I know it's been years. I had wanted to do it long ago but was afraid of Sal's reaction. I know that you don't even know me. I've since remarried and had two more children, but if you ever need an ear I'm here. Once again, my condolences to you and your family.

Regards,
Amanda

Pauline re-read the letter before handing it to Joseph, one of her sons who was helping to write out the thank you notes. They both looked at one another in disbelief. Sal held grudges, that was for sure. It didn't surprise her that he hadn't mentioned this. He never mentioned his military or war experiences. What was astounding was that not only was Sal seeing his best friend on the Other Side as he was dying, Pauline wondered if her mother-in-law helped Miceli in Heaven after the suicide, and that was why Sal was so excited that they had finally met.

With a strong Catholic belief, Pauline knew Sal, just like herself, was taught that suicide was wrong and if you ended your life before your time you would go to Hell. It explained the excitement on Sal's face when he saw his friend.

It was a couple months later when Pauline and Amanda met for lunch, and in a matter of minutes they knew they would be fast and forever friends. They both held a connection and memory to someone they never wanted to let go of.

Deathbed Visions

Bedside visions are quite common, and caretakers and medical staff, especially close-to-end personnel, have witnessed many. Some medical personnel credit medications or a dying brain, seeing as there isn't a scientific explanation for the spiritual phenomenon. I had a physician in my office for a session. He came specifically to alert his wife what a fraud I was and deter her from making such appointments. The session started out interestingly enough when I introduced myself to Joe and my guides immediately told me that Joe wasn't his name, so I called him out on it.

"Joe, or whatever your true name is, but I will call you Joe for this session, have you ever had a reading before?"

My client looked at me sideways and then smirked. "I used a fake name so that you didn't check up on me. My real name is Dale."

"Well, Dale, it's nice to meet the real you. And I'm fine with using a fake name. Many people will use an alias. Or some will send another person other than themselves. I'm fine with whatever."

"So are you going to go Google me now?" Dale laughed.

"Yes, let me tune in to Google," I sarcastically replied. I had no computer in my office, and I certainly had no time to do a check on anybody with my schedule. "What I need you to do is just take a deep breath in and out and then say your name out loud. This is my way of calling on your loved ones."

Dale smacked his lips together, closed his eyes, took a deep breath in and out, and stated his name. He popped his eyes open, looked around and asked me why he couldn't see anybody. I could tell this would was going to be a long fifty minutes.

"Your dad is standing in back of you and he says that he passed suddenly from a heart attack. You were just ten years old, and you were at soccer practice when you found out the news. Aunt Cindy is with him. He says she's the one who picked you up and told you."

Dale furled his brow and looked around, as if trying to find an escape.

"This is why you're here, right? To connect with your loved ones?"

He nodded and swallowed hard.

"He says he's proud of you for becoming a physician, but he's worried that you are burned out. He wants you to consider looking for the possibility of another profession. You won't disappoint anyone, Dale. Not even your mom. She told you that before she passed last year."

Dale stood up and swore at me. "Did my wife call you? Is this a cruel joke?"

I shook my head no, ignored his outburst, and continued to pass along the information his dad was giving me. "Your mom says she loves you and that you did everything for her. The cancer was too aggressive, Dale. She really did see your dad when she was passing, and she hoped that gave you some peace."

"No. No it didn't give me any peace. She didn't really see him and you aren't really seeing them. It's amazing the power of the human brain," Dale explained. "Neurotransmitters and endorphins create hallucinations and auditory disturbances mocking what the patient wants to see and hear, not what they are really seeing or hearing."

"You really believe that?" I asked in awe.

"Yes. Sure, it may give comfort to the family of the dying, but it's not true. It's not real."

I looked at Dale's mom and dad, and they showed me a stethoscope, my sign for the medical field. They were blaming the cynicism on his schooling and training, but the burn out, it made me wonder if he really believed what he was telling me or if he was feeling challenged by what he witnessed and by what he was educated to believe. Show me something that would help, I begged his parents. Something that would be amazing and he could believe.

I didn't know why I wanted to impress Dale so much. I believe that the messages we get are exactly what we are supposed to receive. Sometimes it's so very clear, and sometimes it's hazy. I couldn't predict how the telephone lines to the Other Side would be client to client, or spirit to spirit.

His mom showed me a rosary inside of a white baby shoe and asked me to mention it to him. I had no clue what she was referring to, but I took my chance.

"Dale, your mom is showing me a black pearly rosary that is inside of a baby shoe. Do you know what that is?"

Dale was still standing, and he reached into his coat pocket and pulled out a baby shoe. Inside of the baby shoe was a black pearly rosary. As he dangled the necklace, he gave me a hard look before he asked if I knew the significance.

"Your mom said that the rosary was inside her wedding bouquet when she married your dad and that she held it when she passed away. It was her way to be close to your dad up until the end. The shoe ... something about a private joke."

Dale snickered and finally sat down. "My dad loved Van Gogh. Van Gogh depicted shoes as a sign of struggle, specifically in his 1886 painting entitled 'A Pair of Shoes.' My dad always kept a baby shoe in his car to remember how far he'd gotten. When he passed, I asked for the shoe, and I keep it in my car to remember the same."

I looked over at Dale's dad, whose energy had turned sullen. Then it dawned on me the message. "Dale, you need to paint. Not houses, but pictures. Now, don't quit your day job yet, but there's a calling for you. You're an artist, and that's what the shoe represents to you!"

Dale's attitude also changed when I hit the nerve. Instead of being defensive, he turned into that ten-year-old boy still looking for acceptance from his parents. "Your mom told you over and over that she was proud of you no matter what you did. And she still is. So is your dad. It's okay if you don't believe in them or in your mom's deathbed visions. They still believe in you. Now, did you want to book an appointment for your wife?"

Dale grinned and nodded. "Can I give you a hug?" he asked.

"Of course," I replied. I often hugged my clients after, and sometimes even before, the session. I had pieces of their loved one's energy around me and it was my way of sharing it back.

On the way out the door, Dale turned to me and said, "Kristy, I really do believe Mom saw Dad, but I couldn't wrap my head around how she could see him. I tried to find logical reasoning, but maybe not everything has logic to it and it just is."

I saw Dale a year later for a follow-up session. Although he was still practicing medicine, he had enrolled in some art classes with hopes of using an art form as therapy to help soothe those who are dying.

Shirley Temple

I receive a lot of inquiries about spirits of children visiting those who are dying, but there is one little girl in particular that I've had many describe similarly, and they tell me that she looks a bit like Shirley Temple, the iconic child actress with the ringlet curls. The e-mail below is similar to frequent correspondences that I receive from the family members of someone on the brink of passing.

Kristy,

I'm so sorry to bother you, but my mom is in hospice and her days are few. She wakes up from her many naps describing a little girl who looks like Shirley Temple surrounded in a bright white light. She says the girl's hair is curly and has bows in it. She doesn't say anything, she just sits in the corner and smiles at my mom. I wish I could say this is giving her peace, but it isn't. She doesn't know this little girl, and I don't see what she's seeing. Should she be afraid?

Worried,
Marsha

I replied back that this little girl was either an angel or a Spirit Guide trying to help her mom with the passing. I didn't feel that her mom was concerned about the little girl as much as the little girl taking her to the Other Side and leaving her daughter behind. I suggested that Marsha call on Archangel Michael (or having her mom call on him) to help assist with her fears. I also suggested that they call on familiar loved ones who were on the Other Side to step forward and help bring comfort and peace.

Two days later, I received a response that she took the advice. The little girl remained, but her mom informed Marsha that she could see her parents and her sister who died when she was in her early twenties. A few hours later, Marsha's mom passed away.

Barney

Ken's dad, Eli, served in the Korean War and was a proud man. He wasn't a warm and fuzzy man, but he was extremely caring. He was the type of man that everyone in the family, neighborhood, and town knew they could rely upon for pragmatic and honest advice. When Eli was diagnosed with bone cancer, he knew there'd be no surviving. Although he went through his treatments and never complained about the pain, he understood that he was simply buying time.

One day, Ken had a particularly difficult visit with his dad. He could tell that Eli was suffering and to see his father experience that was emotionally taxing. Ken came home and instantly fell asleep on the couch while watching television.

"It was like my soul left my body," Ken explained to me. "I can't explain it, but all of a sudden I could touch my family room ceiling and then I was transported to the hospital room, where I saw my mom and sister crying. My dad saw me standing in the corner and took my hand. He's never taken my hand before, but he looked at me with such a peaceful smile on his face that I knew he had no more pain. In that moment, it took all of my sadness away seeing him with so much peace that I could actually feel it. All of a sudden

I was in a dark tunnel with a bright light at the end of it with my dad, and when we got to the end, my dad stopped and told me that he had to go. That his family and Barney were waiting for him. He promised to watch over me and the rest of the family, I felt him let go of my hand, and just as he walked in to the light, I woke up to the phone ringing.

I didn't say anything, just nodded in response.

"Of course, it was the call from my mom and sister telling me that my dad had just passed. He told them that he could see Barney in the corner of the room and that he had to go. They said when he passed he had the most peaceful smile on his face. Well, Kristy, Barney was my dad's friend from the war. They had lost touch over the years, but my dad would tell all kinds of stories that included him. I went to look Barney up and found out that he passed a year before, on the exact same day that my dad passed away. What a coincidence," Ken exclaimed.

"Not a coincidence at all," I told him. There are only synchronicities in life.

Letting Go

One of my friends owns a hospice facility on a historic piece of property that overlooks acres of trees and nature. One of her patients was Mary, a lady in her nineties who had her wits about her but her body was beginning to give out. Her entire family, including her own children, had all crossed over, and she was the only one left to make the transition. But she was stubborn. Mary would clench her rosary in her hands and, instead of asking God to take her, she would beg him to save her.

"Who are all these people in my room?" she would complain. "Tell them to go!" she demanded.

Only there were no people in her room that anyone could see. The unseen visitors became even more frequent, and she started complaining that she was awoken to bright white lights shining in her eyes. They then switched to bright blue lights, and they were making her mad. "Why am I being disturbed?" she would cry.

One day when I was visiting my friend at her facility, I felt the energy shift and an angelic presence surrounded me. "There are angels here," I told my friend. "Someone is about to pass."

My friend nodded and shared Mary's experiences. I suggested that she call the Catholic priest soon to see her, as I felt there was unfinished business that she needed to say. Before leaving, I stopped to see Mary to see if there was something that I might be able to assist with.

I was barely in the room, Mary's eyes still closed, when she called out for me to have a seat. I pulled up a chair next to her bed. A patchwork quilt covered her body. Mary opened her eyes and looked at me through thick cataracts. "Do you see them?"

I did, and I told her that I did. In the corner of the room stood several angels along with her family. "They want you to go with them, Mary. Why are you so afraid?"

Mary began to cry, twisting her head from side to side, as if trying to shake out the memories.

"You are forgiven, Mary. I hope you know that. Whatever you are holding on to, you are forgiven."

Mary sighed deeply and shut her eyes for another nap.

Later that evening, the priest came to see Mary. For an hour they talked, Mary confessed her sins, received absolution, and, while the priest held her hand and continued to pray, Mary passed away.

The Heaven Helpers

Many who are dying speak of seeing a light, angels, kids, and familiar people standing in the corner. Sometimes, like for Mary and for Marsha's mom, it can elicit confusion, but other times there's a beautiful feeling of peace that comes from the Heaven helpers.

Billy's father was dying from cancer. It had been days since his dad and favorite fishing buddy had opened his eyes and weeks since he had uttered a word. Billy knew that his dad didn't want to live like that. His dad and he had had the conversation years back while sitting on the dock at their cottage in northern Michigan.

"I don't want you or anyone else putting a diaper on me and changing it. I want to die with dignity," Bill Senior told his son.

It had only been one month since his dad was diagnosed with lung cancer. He'd never even smoked a cigarette in his life and he'd worked an office job. The family was stunned. Billy took a leave from his work and told his family that he had to spend every moment with his dad, especially seeing that his mom was also not well. He knew that his dad would've done the same for him. He placed the hospital bed next to the window that looked out over his dad's spacious yard that he had so carefully taken care of.

"The lawn has to be cut a different way each time it's cut," Bill Senior educated.

Billy's mom would laugh and tell him that all that mattered was that the lawn was cut. She didn't care which way the lines were going, but it mattered to Bill.

Billy heard his dad take a deep breath. He sat up in his bed, opened his eyes, stared into the corner of the room for just a few seconds, and pointed at the ceiling. He turned his head and smiled at Billy, laid back down, and passed away.

Billy sat there stunned, unsure of what had just happened. Just as soon as his dad took his last breath, a bright white light appeared in the corner his dad had looked at and Billy heard in his head his father say, "I love you. Tell Mom I'll be here when she comes."

It was just a few months after Billy lost his dad when his mom took a turn for the worst and passed. Billy said it was from a broken heart. They rarely did anything without the other. Both of his parents were competitive, and he was certain his mom was giving his dad hell for beating her there. Before Billy's mom passed away, she too lay in the same bed Bill Senior had, and although she didn't sit up and point, for a couple weeks before her passing she would look to the corner and smile.

"She sees her Heaven helpers," the hospice nurse told Billy.

"The what?" he queried.

"It's something we see often in our line of work. Those dying see people they know and sometimes those they don't know. These helpers simply wait to deliver them to the Other Side."

The Cross Over

Just as we are delivered in birth, it seems we are delivered in death to a new birth. Our Heaven helpers, the often revolving team of relatives, friends, guides, angels, and other helpers, assist in the delivery. I once had a dying client tell me that she was worried about being stuck.

"Why is that?" I questioned.

"I'm not sure I was loved enough for anyone to help me," she solemnly replied.

My heart broke. As I read for her, though, I saw several people standing around her, all with love. I named them in a roll call type of a way.

Her face lit up and the anxiety that she had about her crossing was replaced with peace. I received an e-mail from her daughter a after her mom passed.

Kristy,

Mom passed away last night. She gazed at the corner of the room and broke into a huge smile. She was content and happy, accepting of her death, even excited about her re-birth into the afterlife.

Ellen

Levels of Afterlife: The Heaven Chronicles

My guides and those on the Other Side have explained to me that there are several levels to the Other Side. Not a physical place, but a spiritual plane where our souls can advance when we are vibrationally aligned, all through free will.

The Cross Over

Once the physical body dies, the soul and spirit leave the body to take its journey to the Other Side. Some have described it as a long tunnel, others as a bright white light. Some see a stairwell, and yet others describe it as a doorway. Just as we have free will and free choice here on Earth, the free will continues to step into the unknown of the light.

The Soul Review

A Soul Review, or Life Review, occurs after we cross over. This involves watching your life and all those you've encountered and impacted, all the actions you've done—the good and bad. It is a teaching tool to understand that life, and death, is to be lived consciously.

Angel Boot Camp

After the Soul Review you get to make the decisions as to what is next. Some choose to quickly reincarnate and others decide to take time to reflect. Some decide to do what is called a soul split, which is leaving a piece of the soul in Heaven and incarnate another piece. Those who decide to stick around choose what their Heaven is and who it includes, as long as it coincides with the other soul.

There aren't any clocks or time on the Other Side, but from an earthly plane explanation, this step takes six to twelve months, which gives their loved ones time to unpack, get settled, and find their voice once more. After all, without a physical body, we don't have vocal chords to talk, right? We are also given an opportunity to help others. This may come as the means of being someone's Spirit Guide or a loved one's Guardian. It could also be an occupation in Heaven, but whatever it is will be something you choose and you will love. You won't ever get that "do I really have to get up in the morning?" feeling here.

Living in Heaven

If a soul hasn't reincarnated, then this is when living occurs, really living. You spend time with those you want to spend time with and do what makes you the most happy, with so much joy. Heaven exists all around the living. It isn't a place like we think of in the earthly sense.

Thank You

Bonnie was born severely physically and mentally handicapped, never learning to speak except for grunts, groans, and moans. She was only twenty-two years old, but her body looked to be eighty, and she was dying. Her parents were told she wouldn't live past eight years of age, but Bonnie defied all predictions. Until now. Her lungs were filled with pockets of infection and one lung had already collapsed. Her kidneys were failing and it was a matter of time before her heart simply stopped beating. The doctors told them that there was nothing else they could do besides make her comfortable. The end would be very soon. So Bonnie's parents Andy and Libby, sat vigil over Bonnie to say their final good-bye.

"Go get dinner," the nurse urged Andy and Libby. "I will page you if there's any change."

Hesitant to leave, but in need of some fresh air, Libby nodded. "I love you, Bon Bon," she said as she leaned over to Bonnie to give her a kiss on the cheek. She promised they'd be back within the hour.

The nurse knew that it was more than likely that Bonnie would pass that day. She had seen the signs and had a sense about it as well, having worked in the intensive care unit for more than ten years. As she tucked the blankets in around her patient, Bonnie's eyes fluttered open.

"Thank you," Bonnie whispered to the nurse.

Unsure that she really heard words, and not just forceful breathing of the one lung, she asked Bonnie if she said something. Bonnie nodded.

"Thank you," Bonnie repeated.

"You're welcome, Bonnie," the nurse replied, stunned. She knew that Bonnie had never spoken and she was in shock. She ran out into the hall to see if she could catch Bonnie's parents, but the hallway was empty except for a resident who had also been caring for Bonnie. "You have to come with me," she said, steering him toward Bonnie's room. "She talked."

"You do need some sleep," the resident laughed.

The nurse guided the resident next to Bonnie's bed, where her eyes were heavy, but open. "Is there anything I can get you, Bonnie?" the doctor asked.

Bonnie slowly shook her head. "Thank you," she said in response.

Just then, Bonnie's parents came back in. Libby ran over to her daughter's side, tears already streaming down her cheek as she laid her head in Bonnie's lap. "Did she ...? I knew I shouldn't have left! I love you, Bonnie. Forever."

Andy, noticing that Bonnie had not slipped away, grabbed his wife's elbow and urged her to look up.

"Oh, Bonnie, I love you!" Libby sobbed in relief.

"Thank you," Bonnie replied with a smile, took a deep breath in, and passed.

The room was still. Andy and Libby were in disbelief at both Bonnie's words and at the graceful passing. They were the only words that they had ever heard her utter, and they were spoken at her death.

Medical journals call it the final surge of energy. Before a person passes, there is a seemingly remarkable recovery. Those who haven't spoken due to disabilities or coma begin to communicate. Those who haven't been responsive react, sit up in bed, and start talking. These surges can last for a few hours to a few days. Although the grieving family's first instinct is to believe that the physical body is miraculously healed. Unfortunately, it's instead the surge of energy to help the dying with their final physical good-bye and to help give the extra boost to their spirit and soul in order to make the spiritual journey.

It was only a few months after Bonnie's passing when Andy and Libby came to see me. The first words their daughter gave as a message were the same as her last words. *Thank you.*

Home

Calvin had been ill for a week. He assumed he had a stomach bug, so he would go to class and then back to his college dorm, where he tried sleeping it off. His roommate was worried about him and kept urging him to call his mom or go to the clinic, but Calvin refused.

It was the ninth night of being ill when Calvin's roommate found him unresponsive, laying on the futon that they so often sat on while playing video games. He called 911, paramedics rushed him to the local hospital, and then he called Calvin's mom and dad, who were several hours away from the campus. They said they'd be there as soon as they could get there.

Calvin was still unresponsive at the hospital, but the emergency doctor knew immediately from his symptoms that Calvin's appendix had ruptured. Before his parents could get there, they rushed him into the operating room.

"We think he'll be okay," the surgeon told Calvin's parents. "It's going to be touch and go for a few days, and this is quite serious, but we are hopeful."

Calvin was a great kid. He was smart and on a full scholarship to the state university. He'd played football and wrestled in high school, but he wanted to spend his energy pursuing his career in engineering. Every time he called home, he would talk about the intern opportunities that he was being offered for the following year. "I feel good about this," he'd say.

His parents were proud of him, and although they missed him, they loved Calvin's zest for life and unapologetic independence. He'd always been super healthy too, so this medical emergency was odd to them.

Calvin lay in the Intensive Care Unit. His body, hooked to the many tubes, looked small and frail in the bed. It's a sight to see for anybody, but Calvin's mom was concerned. Something didn't feel right, and she mentioned it to her husband, the nurse, and the doctor, but they all reassured her that he was okay—he just had to heal.

The next day, they removed the tubes except for one in the stomach, which is helping to release an infection. Calvin opened his eyes, confused and medicated. He asked his mom if his bags were packed. She replied that she would go get him some clothes and such, but that he was okay for now. He seemed agitated.

"I don't have my bags packed yet. I need to get my things together to go home!" he told his mom.

"Yes, hon, we will get there in due time," she comforted.

Calvin fell asleep, but woke up an hour later. "I think I found the map to home, Mom. I love you."

"I love you too, Calvin. We'll get you home."

Calvin shook his head no and fell back asleep, but he never woke up. The infection had been too much for his heart and he went into cardiac arrest and passed away.

Calvin's mom requested to say a few words at the funeral, despite everyone telling her it would be too hard.

"Calvin told me that he needed to get home. I thought he meant back to college or back to his family home, but I now know that he mean he needed to go back to his spiritual home. He was a gift to me, and although those nineteen years were short and I selfishly wish it were more, I know that he found the map back to his true and real home—Heaven. I also know that he is doing some incredible things over there and one day I will find home too and join him. Until then, I will treasure the years I was gifted."

Hospice nurses and those who are around the dying often claim that the patients talk about needing to go home. Sometimes it is misinterpreted as they want to be in their home, their own bed, and sometimes this is the case. Yet more often they mean their heavenly home. My mom spoke of going home before her passing. She could see her relatives waiting for her and said she just wanted to go home. When I told her we were trying to get her there, she told me that wasn't the home she meant, she meant *home*, and emphasized the word. She found her way soon after.

Chapter Nine

After Death Visits

Plenty of people have experienced a visit from their loved one soon after their death, and before the knowledge they'd expired.

Years ago, I was reading for a young man who told me that he was primarily there to talk about work, but I always allow spirit to communicate what they want to. Most times that is the best message we receive, and the worries on our mind resolve on their own.

"Lee, I have someone here who says he's your brother. He said he passed in a tragic automobile accident. I want to say that his name is Michael. He's super tall, maybe over six-four, with brown hair. In fact, he says that his mop top was a private joke. He was always good with his hands and shows me a blue collar, which is a sign that he worked in the industrial trade."

Lee looked at me oddly, which isn't abnormal. People come to see me, and sometimes I'm not certain what they are expecting, because they are surprised when I make the connections. So instead of asking Lee why the strange look, I continued on.

"Your mom is also here. She said she helped your brother cross over. She said she passed from cancer, some form of girly cancer, ovarian or cervical. She's been passed for more than ten years and she knows you miss her. She shows me a wedding ring, and says that Dad is still here. She still loves him very much."

I looked over at Lee, who was still staring at me.

"Are you okay?" I asked.

"Yes. No. Well, maybe," Lee stammered. "Everything you said about Mom is right, but my brother is still here, alive and well. And yes, his name is Michael, and he works for Chrysler, which is industrial. But, I just spoke to him this morning and he's here."

I looked over again at who I saw as Lee's brother in spirit and he was still standing there. *Maybe I'm tired,* I tried to reason. Or maybe there was someone else on the Other Side who was close to Lee's brother who passed away. I saw Michael shake his head no at me, but I was trying to find a reason why I was seeing him on the Other Side. I didn't see living people, I just sensed them. That is unless they were about to pass or there was some sort of neurological problem, like Alzheimer's. But nope, Michael was standing there and saying that the lady I was communicating with was his mom just as she was Lee's mom.

"So can we talk about my work now?" Lee asked.

I just didn't feel as if I was wrong, or that a hitchhiker spirit snuck in. There are no coincidences, after all. Lee was my client, though, so I moved away from Michael and his message and to the area he wanted assistance with.

The session ended and Lee seemed satisfied. We said our goodbyes. After he left, I shut the door to my office and started to shut off the lights and blow out the candles, as he was my last client of the day. I turned my phone on and heard the familiar jingle of some text messages coming through, so I grabbed my jacket off the rack, put it on, and sat down to make sure there weren't any emergencies. That's when I heard the gentle knock on my door. I thought it was probably my friend Gayle coming to say hi since her office was across the hallway and she probably noticed that my client left. When I opened the door, instead of Gayle standing there, it was Lee. His face was ashen.

"Kristy …" he stammered, "I just got off the phone with my dad."

I guided him to sit down. I was afraid he was going to pass out the way he was shaking.

"My brother was killed in a car accident about an hour ago, Kristy!"

"Oh my …," I sputtered. "I'm so sorry!"

"Can you get him back, Kristy? Can you talk to him again?"

I texted my husband that I'd be late coming home and I started the session all over again. Unfortunately I couldn't reach his brother, but his mom did come through with messages regarding what happened and informed us that Michael was still making his transition, but he was okay.

Now if I see someone on the Other Side and the client tells me that I'm describing a person, only they are still alive in a physical sense, I admit that I get concerned.

Can't Stay Long

"Dad, what are you doing here?"

Renee got up off the ground where she was weeding her flower bed and dusted off her knees.

Fred had been in the hospital for the past few weeks fighting pneumonia, and with his COPD and previous heart conditions, Renee was startled to see her dad walking up her driveway toward her.

"I was just about to call Mom to see how you were doing. Wait, where's Mom, Dad?" Renee looked around him, not seeing her parents' white Buick.

"It's just me, hon. I just wanted to tell you that I love you." Her dad was wearing his baggy jeans and flannel coat, which he wore whether it was twenty degrees below zero or a hundred outside.

"I love you too, Dad," Renee replied, confused by the impromptu visit. "Here, take a seat on the bench, and I'll get us some lemonade." *And call Mom,* she said to herself.

Her dad nodded, all the while continuing to smile. "I can't stay long."

Renee rushed into the house. Just as she grabbed her cell phone, it rang. The number on the display was the hospital number that she'd called several times since the day her dad was admitted. Renee's life was chaotic and sometimes she wasn't able to visit, but she always called to make sure her dad was doing okay. She had plans to visit him that day, but time escaped her and last night when she checked up on him her mom said he'd been doing great. He was joking and sitting in a chair, her mom announced, and complaining about the food. He was excited that the doctors said he would probably be home by week's end. *By week's end,* she repeated in her head. That was still five days from now. Maybe Dad escaped from the hospital, Renee panicked and answered the call.

"Renee, its Bobby," she heard her brother say on the other end. "I think you better get to the hospital. Dad's taken a turn for the worst, and well ...," Bobby hesitated and started to cry into the phone. "Renee, Dad died a few minutes ago."

Startled, she started laughing. *No, no, he's on my front porch. He must've had a great escape from Saint Anthony's hospital. What a funny time they will have when telling this story during the holidays.*

"Bobby, that's ridiculous. Dad is on my front porch. I'm getting him a drink right now."

"What are you talking about? Dad's passed away, Renee. Mom is calling the funeral home now to make the arrangements to pick his body up, but she wanted you to come here first to say your good-bye."

Renee dropped the phone on the counter with Bobby still on the other end. She heard a car door slam shut and moments later her husband walked into the house. Rushing to the door, she greeted him. "Tom, did you see Dad sitting on the bench out there?"

"Your dad? Isn't he still in the hospital? Nobody is sitting on the porch," Tom answered.

"Renee! Renee, are you still there?" Bobby yelled through the phone.

"Who's on the phone?" Tom asked, confused.

Renee pushed past Tom to where she left her dad, but there wasn't anyone sitting there.

"I know he was here. I know he was," Renee frantically muttered to herself.

"Tom," she yelled from the front yard, "we have to go search for Dad."

By the time Renee made it into the house, Tom had already spoken to Bobby and heard the sad news. He told him they'd be on the way to the hospital soon and grabbed Renee by the shoulders to steady her.

"Let's go to the hospital first, Renee. I think that is what's best." Tom gently took Renee by the hand, locked up the house, and guided her into the car.

"I saw him, Tom. I really did."

Tom nodded in silence.

Renee's dad lay in his hospital bed, dead. Renee looked at Bobby, her mom, and then to Tom and back to her dad. She ambled up to her dad's body, bent over, and gave him a kiss on his cheek. "I love you too, Dad," she whispered. "Thank you for the good-bye."

Continue On

Physical visits afterward aren't as rare as many would think. Many have reported being shaken awake at night and seeing their loved one on the Other Side standing there looking translucent, but still in a physical form. Others have heard their name being called, in both sleep and awake states, with a familiar voice from a loved one on the Other Side.

Chapter Ten

Knocking on Heaven's Door

Presley had a bit of a bad boy persona from the time he was very young. He was the type of kid who would jump off the roof if someone dared him to. His sister, Barb, was the complete opposite —very cautious and careful with everything in her life—but Barb and Presley were best friends in childhood and into adulthood, too.

Their parents had died when they were both in their early twenties and all they had was one another. Presley was a bit bitter about it. Barb would tell her friends and husband that Presley took chances because he was too busy and didn't think things through.

It was a spring evening when Barb received the call from Presley's flavor of the month that they'd had a motorcycle accident and he was in critical condition in the hospital. The doctors needed first of kin immediately. She knew that didn't sound good.

Barb and her husband drove as fast as they could to the hospital. To be honest, she didn't even remember the drive, she just remembered praying and asking her mom and dad not to take her only brother, her only sibling too. But there were other plans than the ones she wanted, and by the time she got to the hospital Presley had died.

The first day of the visitation for Presley's funeral had been a busy one, with a constant flow of friends and family coming through. Presley had a huge circle of love around him, and everyone had a story to share. Barb sat on the couch in front of the casket that held her brother's body and closed her eyes. All of a sudden she felt Presley standing next to her and she heard him say, "Love ya, sis. Later, gator." She opened her eyes and nobody was there. Then she heard three distinct knocks. *Weird,* she thought. *Maybe the air conditioning is coming on,* she discounted.

Her husband was sitting in the lobby with their kids when she came out. She asked if anyone had come into the room, and they all shook their heads no.

"Did you hear those three loud knocks?" she asked.

Again, they shook their heads no.

The night before his funeral, Barb had a vivid dream with her brother in it. She was sitting next to him at the hospital, but he was alive, and they were watching a Detroit Tigers game. Presley was yelling at the pitching staff.

"For crying out loud, I can pitch better than that, you loser!" he screamed.

Barb laughed. Presley didn't have a filter on his mouth, and he was okay with it.

"Hey, sis," Presley said. "It's time for you to go. Love ya, sis. Later, gator."

Barb woke up with a start. It was so real and it shook her. It was only two in the morning, but she got up to get a glass of milk when she heard three distinct knocks on her front door.

Startled by the knocking, and wondering who could possibly be at her front door in the middle of the night, she woke up her husband. He checked, but nobody was there.

"I swear I heard three knocks!" she told him.

With hardly any sleep, Barb got ready for the funeral, feeling drugged and comatose from the exhaustion and grief. She couldn't get the knocks out of her head and was afraid to mention it again to her husband, for fear he'd think she was truly going insane.

The funeral was so packed that it was standing room only. It was a rock star funeral and the luncheon was more like a celebration, something she knew Presley would've loved. One of Presley's old girlfriends came up to Barb as everyone was leaving. Barb always loved Tricia, and she had hoped that her brother would've settled down with her.

"I'm so sorry, Barb. I know Presley loved and cared for you very much," Tricia said with a hug.

Barb just nodded.

"Can I tell you something weird, though? I hope you don't think I'm crazy," Tricia continued on.

"Sure," Barb said, now curious.

"I was sleeping last night and woke up to a bunch of knocking on my front door!" Tricia exclaimed. "Nobody was there, but it scared me because it was two in the morning. Something, though, told me that it was Pres telling me good-bye."

Barb stood there with her mouth hanging open.

Barb shared her own incidences and felt validated that Presley was surely saying his good-bye.

There's a legend that if you hear three loud knocks someone close to you is going to die, and if you hear four knocks it's a bad spirit and don't open the door. Now, this is an old legend and not necessarily true. Presley had already passed away, but Barb believed he hadn't yet crossed over. He never followed the rules. He did what he wanted to do, when he wanted to do it. Barb believed it was Presley's final good-bye.

Sometimes Barb still hears the knocks from Heaven, as she calls them. It no longer scares her, as she knows that it's Presley trying to get her attention.

Knocking or ringing of the doorbell is common after-death communication. It usually happens soon—minutes or days—after death.

It's NOT All In Your Head

Our loved ones can communicate using sound. Sometimes the sound is physical, and other times it is manifested telepathically, like hearing the voice or a noise in your head.

The louder the spirit was on this earthly plane, the louder they will be on the Other Side. We don't change our personality. So it made perfect sense that Presley, a loud and boisterous person in life, would knock three times. He demanded to be heard, and he was.

There is a male spirit in my office building. He was there before I moved in, and he causes no problems except he flushes the toilet. Not one that has a sensor on it either, but the good, old-fashioned, push down the handle kind. Often it will be an evening or a week-end day and I will be with my client and we will hear *flush* in the women's restroom and nobody is there. Except for the ghost we call Richard, aka the toilet-flushing bandit. He just wants his presence recognized, and then he continues on his way.

Voices from Beyond

Deceased loved ones and angels are indeed watching over us. There are numerous reports of people who've received protection from criminal activity, potential auto accidents, fires, undiagnosed health problems, and more. Have you ever heard a voice in your head telling you "Slow down" or "Take a different exit" only to realize later that you avoided an accident? Or "Call your loved one" and found out they were in need of some help? Always trust the voices in your head.

Common Noises That Spirit Share

- Voices
- Your name being called
- Footsteps
- Period music
- Dogs barking
- Birds chirping
- Knocking
- The sound of furniture or something heavy being moved
- High-pitched noise in your ear
- Buzzing in your ear
- Sound of a doorknob jingling
- Sound of keys on a key ring
- Wind chimes
- Bells ringing
- Dishes rattling in the kitchen

Chapter Eleven

Before Your Time

It's always hard to lose someone you love, especially when there isn't any closure. At the hands of suicide, there are a multitude of emotions that the griever experiences, as does the spirit.

I was raised to believe the Bible stated that if you commit suicide it becomes a one-way ticket to Hell. Although I believe there are other positive options rather than suicide, I have never had anyone come to me in spirit and tell me that because of their suicide they ended up in a fiery pit. I have, however, had many who've taken their life and communicated their regret.

Suicide is not the answer, but it happens. Those who've gone to the Other Side before their time, by means of suicide, have to attend to the issues they thought they might escape through their final action. It's a soul searching that can be done here or there, it's part of our choice. A troubled soul who can only see the storm clouds doesn't automatically see the sunshine once the heart stops beating. That memory of pain and sadness is part of the soul. It's a darkness that our angels and guides try to help here in the physical as much as they try and help on the other side.

Those who cross over from suicide are, though, greeted by their loved ones and given the opportunity to heal through that darkness, but oftentimes the guilt from their last action leaves them in a place of sadness that they had before they left. They are given opportunities to continue to heal and to try and heal those they've left and those they've hurt.

If you've lost a loved one to suicide, keep talking to them. As you forgive, they too may begin to forgive themselves, releasing their own chains of emotion.

He's In Heaven

"We'd had a horrible fight that morning," Sadie explained. "He didn't answer my texts or calls after school, so I assumed he was still angry. It was seriously over him taking the trash out, but Luke held grudges, and I guess he'd been having a hard time. Fifteen-year-olds, you know?"

Sadie came to see me on a wintry day in Michigan. I tried to postpone her appointment for fear of the weather and her safety, but she would have none of it. She wanted to come even if there was a blizzard. I could see Luke, her son, in spirit standing next to her. He felt remorseful, and when he told me his side of the story, I couldn't help but feel emotional.

"He says he hung himself after you left for work that morning."

Sadie sighed. "That's what the coroner said too. I sure wish the school had called to tell me he didn't show up, but then there's a lot of should've, could've, and would'ves that I have. I should've just taken the trash out. I could've not made such a big deal about it. It would've changed everything."

Luke began to cry on the Other Side. It was the first anniversary of his passing, he said. And he had a whole lot of regrets, too.

"He's in Heaven, Sadie, he's just sad he's made everyone so sad." Luke showed me a fuzzy dog with floppy ears with him and then brought through a young girl who looked to be about sixteen years old. Her hair was light brown and long, and she had beautiful blue eyes. I told Sadie who was with Luke, and although she recognized the dog as Barkley, she didn't know who the girl was.

"No, she won't," Luke told me. "I met her here and fell in love. I supposed she's a match made in Heaven. After our training here, we are going to be in charge of a children's group."

Sadie gave me a strange look when I shared Luke's message. "Do you know the girl's name?" Sadie asked me.

"Her name is Rachel," Luke said.

Sadie told me that ever since Luke was a small boy all he'd talked about was getting married and having a family. It wasn't necessarily a normal thing for a young boy to aspire for, but Sadie said it was Luke's dream. "He would've made an amazing teacher."

"I think that's exactly what he's doing," I shared.

Several months later, I had a woman come for a session. As soon as she sat down, Luke and Rachel came through. "This is very strange," I said. "Your daughter is here, and I think I've met her before through another reading."

My client looked confused, so I continued on. Rachel had also committed suicide, around the time Luke had. Although they didn't attend the same school, they had lived just a few cities apart.

"Do you mind if I give Sadie your phone number? I realize this is odd."

But Rachel's mom didn't think it was odd at all. "Rachel came to me in a dream, I guess you call it a visit, with a young man. I had no idea who he was. I suppose the mystery is solved."

A week later, Luke's and Rachel's moms met for lunch. It's now been several years since their kids passed, and their moms remain the best of friends. It was a match made in Heaven for all parties, and although they all wish Luke and Rachel were still here, they are glad that they both came to see me and were introduced.

That was the first time I'd ever seen or heard about relationships from strangers being formed on the Other Side. I thought it was a beautiful reminder that even on the Other Side we interact, befriend others, and can fall in love.

Suicide Is Not the Answer

Suicide is not the answer. It is never the answer. But we have to be realistic: it happens. When I receive inquiries from those contemplating suicide and inquiries whether or not they will go to a good place if they go through with it, I tell them the truth. I am never sure, and because of that uncertainty, why would they take the gamble? Instead it is best to look for help and healing here.

If you are having suicidal thoughts, you're not alone; many have had suicidal thoughts at some point in their lives. Feeling suicidal is not a character defect, and it doesn't mean that you are crazy or weak. It only means that you have more pain than you can cope with at that point in time. The pain may seem permanent, but with time and support, the pain and the suicidal thoughts can be healed. Here are some places you can turn to:

In the United States—Call the National Suicide Prevention Lifeline at 1-800-273-TALK (8255) or the National Hopeline Network at 1-800-SUICIDE (1-800-784-2433). These toll-free crisis hotlines offer twenty-four–hour suicide prevention and support. Your call is free and confidential. You can also chat with someone at the Suicide Prevention Lifeline at suicidepreventionlifeline.org.

Outside the United States—Visit International Association for Suicide Prevention (www.iasp.info) or suicide.org to find a helpline in your country.

Chapter Twelve

Unfinished Business

"Please, for Dawn's wedding," Callie would beg her husband.

"I've got two left feet and would probably break yours. You know how exciting dancing sounds to me, Cal," Scott whined.

They were just two months shy of their eldest daughter's wedding and Callie wanted to impress the guests with some ballroom dancing moves. Her favorite show, *Dancing with the Stars,* also helped to rouse the urgent request.

Callie had been asking Scott to take lessons from Arthur Murray since before they were married almost thirty years before. She knew it was a long shot, but she tried anyhow, unsuccessfully. Not wanting to start a fight, she simply dropped it.

"Nope, I can't seem to convince him, Dawn," she told her daughter. "He's incredibly stubborn."

Dawn was disappointed as well. She had visions of the most perfect father-daughter dance. At her wedding rehearsal dinner the Wednesday before the Saturday wedding, she voiced her dismay, keeping it light. "So, Dad, are you just going to stand there while I dance around you?" Dawn teased.

Scott rolled his eyes, "Not you too. I can dance, I'm just not Fred Astaire, nor do I want to be. I'm simply your dad. Isn't that good enough?" he teased back.

Dawn, her mom, and the guests laughed. Dawn walked over and planted a big kiss on the top of her dad's head.

On the drive home from dinner, Scott turned the radio off. "Cal, I hope I haven't disappointed you or Dawn by not taking dancing lessons. I probably should've and it was my stupid pride for not—"

Before Scott could finish his sentence, a pickup truck ran a stop sign and broadsided their vehicle. Scott died immediately. While Scott was being taken to the morgue, Callie was whisked to the hospital with several bumps and bruises, but the worst just a broken arm.

Instead of the wedding party going home for some needed sleep, they spent the night with Dawn in the hospital, as she grieved, worried, and wept. She didn't care about the wedding and called for a postponement. Her fiancé agreed. The next morning her mom was released.

"You're coming home with me," Dawn urged.

"No. No, I want my own bed, Dawn. I want to be in my home," Callie said.

Dawn's tears had hardly stopped since she had received the phone call about the accident the previous night.

"I'm postponing the wedding, Mom. You and—" Dawn's words caught in her throat, "Dad's funeral are the priorities."

Callie once again opposed her daughter. "No, the wedding will go on, Dawn. You know just as I do that Dad would've wanted it that way. He'd feel awful for ruining your day. I know it'll be hard. God, I know," Callie said, beginning to cry, but she quickly gained her composure. "But this is the way he'd want it. With our faith, we know he'll be there in spirit."

The night before the wedding, Callie snuggled into the bed that Scott and she had shared for so many years. She wasn't sure if she'd ever get used to going to bed alone, not hearing Scott yell at the television when his baseball team disappointed him, and countless other trite day-to-days that were now meaningful memories.

"Oh, Scott," she prayed, "please be with us these next couple days, and then I understand if you want to spend your time with your family in Heaven. Right now, though, Dawn and I really need you."

Callie fell asleep, her pillow wet with tears.

"Cal. Cal, wake up."

Callie heard Scott call for her. It was the sorrow playing tricks on her, she thought. *I really hope I never forget the sound of his voice.* The tears began again.

"Cal, I only have a moment. Wake up," Scott urged.

Callie opened her eyes to see her husband standing next to her bed. He was surrounded by the brightest white light she had ever seen. It felt like sunshine on her face after a week of storms.

"You are—"Callie started, but Scott held out his hand to her. Before she grabbed ahold, she first panicked.

"No, it isn't your time, Cal. When it is I will be there, but … will you have this dance?" Scott asked.

Callie got up out of bed and Scott wrapped her in an embrace, careful not to hurt her broken arm, and then took a dancing pose. They then began to dance around the bedroom. With each twirl, Scott would lean over and gently kiss her on her lips.

"I have to go now, Callie," Scott whispered in her ear. "Tell the girls they will always be my little princesses."

Just as soon as Callie was awakened, she found herself snuggled back into her bed, pillow propped under her broken arm. She would've thought it had been just a dream, but she could still feel the tingle of Scott's soft lips on hers.

The next morning was Dawn's wedding day. Although Callie was still mourning, she felt lighter than she had. One of the brides-maids picked her up at the house to take her to the spa where they were all getting ready.

Dawn immediately ran over to her mom when she entered and gave her a hug.

"Mom, Mom!" Dawn exclaimed like an excited five-year-old. "Mom, I had the most amazing dream last night with Dad!"

"I did, too," Callie said, matching Dawn's enthusiasm. "He danced with me," Callie said, tears forming as she thought back to the moment.

"He danced with *me*!" Dawn declared. "He woke me up last night and told me that he still wanted to have our dance. It felt so real!"

Callie knew it was real. It was a special moment that both Dawn and her shared. Although not quite the same as the real thing, it was precious nonetheless.

Beautiful grape hyacinths and yellow roses dotted the church that Saturday afternoon as Callie and Scott's daughter walked down the aisle with just her mom, the sun's rays shone a rainbow of color through the stained glass windows on Dawn and Callie. They both knew they could feel Scott there.

Callie gave Dawn's hand over to her new husband and her new life. A new life for all of them, Callie supposed, but she was grate-ful for her final dance.

Therapists and dream experts believe if you dream about a passed relative or friend that it is a manifestation of guilt or sorrow, but there have been many reports of loved ones having same-night visitations that held eerie similarities.

Here Some Guilt, There Some Guilt, Everywhere Some Guilt … Even in Heaven

Our loved ones often feel guilty as well. The guilt is not just the pain they caused by their death but also because of arguments and disappointments they believe they caused in their life. Some of the things they regret may not even be real in the minds of the living. It's like parent guilt. Often parents feel their kids are upset at them for not being able to make a field trip or a sporting event, when the kids weren't upset at all. Those on the Other Side can also carry worldly weights with them up and through the pearly gate, and the visits are a means for them to ask forgiveness.

Gwen was a client of mine. Her dad passed from a heart condition made worse by his habit of smoking. When he passed away, he would visit her several times a year and simply tell her that he was sorry.

"He was a great dad," she told me one day in my office. "He has nothing to be sorry about!"

Her dad had showed up to Samantha's appointment even before she did. He sat in the corner, patiently waiting, but with a nervous energy.

"She told me to quit. No she begged me to quit smoking for years. I should've taken her advice. I see how sad she is on holidays, Father's Day, birthdays, and opening day of baseball," Saul, Gwen's dad, said.

When I passed along the message, Gwen laughed about the opening day of baseball. "It was probably the most important holiday out of all of them," she explained. "I'm not upset with him, though. He used to say we all have to die some way. He was right."

"Tell her I'm sorry, though," Saul urged.

"I'm not upset about that. I just miss him, that's all."

"Maybe now he won't spend all his visitation time apologizing," I remarked.

"From your mouth to Dad's ears," Gwen smiled.

A few weeks later, I received a call from Gwen telling me that she did in fact have another visit from her dad, and this time he took her to an old baseball stadium where they sat and chatted. "It was like old times," Gwen quipped. "It was nice."

If you receive an *I'm sorry* visit from your loved one, look a bit deeper than the surface of the message. Is there another reason they may think you are upset with them? If there is, maybe it's time to tell them you forgive them, even if for you it isn't a big deal.

Chapter Thirteen

Is There a Pawn Shop in Heaven?

"Kristy, I'm pretty certain that my sister took a Mother's Day ring that I gave to Mom years back. Can you ask her who has it and where it's at?" my client Stephanie asked.

Whether a ring or a rosary, it's amazing how many times a week I'm asked about missing jewelry, especially soon after a passing. It's obvious to assume that a family member snuck in and took liberties with the goods, and although that is sometimes the case, it isn't always.

I looked over at her mom in spirit, who told me that the ring was in her things, not missing at all. It was there.

"I've seriously looked through everything. Even in all of the clothes' pockets. I've checked with the hospital and the funeral home. Nothing. I can't imagine that it's anywhere but with my sister, who denies that she took anything."

"I'm just the messenger, Stephanie. Your mom says it's there." I shrugged.

I receive calls and e-mails on missing objects all of the time, and to be perfectly honest I stink at finding lost objects. I'm the one who loses my keys, phone, rings, and anything else that can get lost, all of the time. Now, lost people, whether alive or deceased, I'm pretty good at finding and the reason is energy. Although human and inanimate objects have energy, it's a different energy and is read unlike how I normally interpret energy. I can ask someone on the Other Side for help in locating an object, but I can't zoom into the energy of the object to find it. It's just not my gift and I explained that to Stephanie.

"That's okay, Kristy," she said exasperatedly. "I understand."

But I could tell that it wasn't okay and she didn't understand, and I felt bad.

A week later, I received a phone call from Stephanie. "I'm so baffled. I had a box of Mom's things in my room and I dropped my earring in it when I was putting it on, so I carefully took out the goods only to find the ring in the corner of the box right next to my earring. What's even more odd is that I was getting ready for my niece's wedding and kept thinking how nice it would be to have something of Mom's with me. How's that, Kristy?"

"Timing is everything, isn't it?" I smiled into the phone.

"I feel horrible for blaming my sister!" Stephanie added, and thanked me again for the session before we ended the conversation.

I'm not sure where the jewelry goes, and the spirits have assured me that there's not a pawn shop in Heaven, but I have found that the timing of finding the lost objects always seems to be the right timing.

Returned Goods

"Hi, I'm Kristy," I said when the man answered the door.

"Oh, you're the psycho, I mean *psychic*. Sorry," he joked.

I rolled my eyes. It wasn't the first time I'd heard the insult, and it wasn't going to be the last time either.

"Ted, just let her in!" I heard Amy call from behind her husband.

Ted resembled Mr. Clean in both looks and stature, with a shiny bald head to boot. I couldn't see Amy at all behind him.

I had met Amy just a couple months back when she came in for a reading. When Ted's mom passed away unexpectedly, she asked if I'd come to the house and talk to the family, and maybe even contact their mom to help with some closure.

Ted opened the door for me and I stepped in. Amy met me with a hug. "Ignore him, Kristy. He thinks he's funny."

I smiled and let her guide me to their family room, where the family was already sitting. With a quick introduction, I reiterated that I usually asked for a one-year wait, but said I'd do my best to make contact. I closed my eyes and dialed the phone to the Other Side, so to speak. Immediately a spunky lady with bright red hair came through. She explained that she was at peace and with her husband. She said she'd been sick for years with a multitude of ailments and had done mostly everything she was supposed to do, well, except for quit smoking, and that her passing, while unexpected in timing shouldn't have been so unexpected with her various health issues. I shared the information and the family nodded and laughed about Annie's stubbornness on not stopping, and swearing that her heart problems weren't at all exasperated by her smokes.

One of the women, who introduced herself as Abby, asked if I could ask her mom a question, and I nodded. "Can you ask her where her jewelry went, Kristy? We've searched high and low and it's as if it just vanished. She had a respiratory nurse that came in several times a week, did she steal it?"

I looked at Annie, who pointed at Ted and then made a shushing motion as if it were a secret. I gave a sideways glance over at Ted, who looked panicked

"She says it's safe and it will turn up once things have settled down."

Annie smiled and nodded that I said the right thing. Ted was still looking like a five-year-old whose hand was caught in the cookie jar.

I continued passing along messages and fielding questions about the Other Side for another forty minutes before saying my good-byes.

"I'll see Kristy out," Ted told his wife and siblings, taking my hand and guiding me out the door. "How did you …?"

"Remember, I'm a psycho, I mean psychic," I answered sarcastically. "Your mom did say that you are going to have to fess up soon, though, because your sister Chris is going to start accusing everybody, and that isn't right either."

"It's Abby that I was worried about. If she had gotten to the jewelry before me, she would've pawned it. I just know she would've. I had to do something. Not even Amy knows I have it, and I feel horrible." Ted rubbed his shiny bald head in despair.

I knew he had good intentions. His mom did too. It was a sticky spot that he was in. I could still feel his mom's energy near him and I asked her for guidance.

"Your mom says to take each piece and put them in individual bags with names of your siblings on it, the way you see fit. Everybody gets something. Everybody. And if Abby pawns it, that's her prerogative. Okay?"

Ted nodded. I could almost see the wheels turning in his head, as if he were taking inventory of each piece and trying to figure out what to give his sister Abby. "I can't give her the wedding ring, though, Kristy. I just can't."

"Nobody said for you to."

"Thank you for not tattling on me. I appreciate it. I'm sorry for calling you a psycho, too."

Ted quickly gave me a hug and a kiss on the cheek and walked inside without a good-bye.

A week later I received an e-mail from Ted's sister, Abby.

Kristy,

It's the darnedest thing, but we found mom's jewelry in a box under her winter sweaters. You were right. Thanks so much!"

Warm Wishes,
Abby

I simply smiled and wished the family well as I deleted the e-mail.

Calm During the Storm

My mom was petrified of storms and would wake me up out of a still sleep to sit with her, which only added to my own fear of storms. When my mom passed away, she left a lot of jewelry. Nothing had of a lot value except the sentimental kind. My dad gave my sister and I all of it. He told us to go through it, keep what we wanted, and take the rest to the pawn shop and bring him back the money. To be honest I was horrified, but some people go through grieving differently.

My mom passed on a Monday, the funeral was on a Thursday, and my dad demanded that we come to the house by Saturday and clean out my mom's closets. It wasn't that he didn't love her, it was just his way of dealing with her death, or not dealing with her death. The more of her stuff out of sight, the more out of mind for him, and he didn't have to mourn. My sister and I each chose a few pieces of jewelry and gathered up the rest to take to the jewelry shop. We came back with a small amount of cash that we handed to Dad, who was dissatisfied that it wasn't more.

One spring evening right after my mom's passing, I was home alone for the night when the tornado sirens went off. Shaking, I grabbed my dog and cat and made my way down into our basement, all the while hearing the howling of the wind and branches hitting the windows. The hue through the basement windows was pea green, never a good sign when there is a storm. The wind continued to gust outside and just as soon as I went to take a seat on the couch, the power flashed off. *Great,* I thought.

Michigan was known for storms, especially in the spring time, and you would've thought I'd have been more prepared with candles and a flashlight, but I wasn't. I didn't even grab my cell phone. I had left it on the kitchen counter upstairs. Remembering that I had a flashlight in a cabinet near where I was, I fumbled around until I found the piece of furniture in the dark and opened the cabinet drawer. Feeling around, instead of a flashlight, my hand touched a piece of jewelry and I picked it up. Just as I held it in my hand, the lights flashed on.

My mom loved rings and her fingers were often adorned with gemstones of all types. In my basement cabinet, I pulled out an amethyst ring that my mom often wore. I was puzzled. The ring hadn't been gifted to me, and I knew that I hadn't seen the ring in my mom's things to keep or to pawn. So how was it here in the basement cabinet? My mom hadn't ever been down in my basement and had only been to my home a couple times. Before I could ponder it anymore, the storm outside calmed and sunshine shone through the windows. I was safe. I would like to think it was my mom's way of calming me during the storm, even if she added an element of mystery to it.

Move It On Over

Have you ever misplaced or lost something only for it to appear exactly where you've looked before? Does a framed photo of a deceased loved one keep falling? Spirit can certainly move objects or place objects in odd places to get our attention.

Chapter Fourteen

You Belong

He stood in my office, looking over my client, his mom. He had short blond hair and piercing blue eyes, and he showed himself wearing white slacks and a white shirt, as if he just stepped out of an angel sequence on television. Although he was handsome, there was an energy about him, as if the sun reflected from within him made him stunning. He said his name was Gil, named after his mom's dad.

"I don't understand. I don't get it. I don't know how he could've killed himself," Lottie said.

Gil fiercely shook his head. "I didn't," he kept saying over and over. "I didn't."

I never wanted to offer false hope, just pass along the messages. What's the old phrase, don't shoot the messenger? That was something I could probably repeat a dozen times a day.

I could tell Gil wasn't telling me everything, and I begged him to give me more.

"Tell her that I'm always watching over her and that I love how much she loves my daughter."

Lottie stared hard at her coffee cup before speaking. "His daughter misses him. She's only eight years old, you know? And without a dad, well, he knows how that is."

Gil nodded in agreement. "Tell her my father has crossed over. She needs to file papers." He showed me legal papers.

"Did you know your ex-husband died?" I asked.

"That jerk better not be here. I refuse to talk to him. He left me and Gil and he doesn't get my time." Lottie said, fired up.

"No, no, he isn't here," I said trying to diffuse the situation. "Your son said you have legal documents to sign. There are some monies coming to you. Maybe call social security," I offered, shrugging.

"Okay," she quietly said. "What about his wife? Why isn't he talking about her?"

I looked over at Gil only for him to turn to the side so I couldn't see his face. That was as difficult for me as a deaf person trying to read lips with the person speaking not facing them. But I understood what he was telling me by his actions. He didn't commit suicide.

Lottie was sharp, and she understood my silence. I looked over at Gil, who now hung his head down. "It was just an unfortunate accident," Gil sighed. "We were fighting and she took out the gun. I tried to stop her from doing something stupid and I got caught with the bullet in my head."

"I knew it," Lottie confirmed. "That's all I need," she said and got up to leave, with a half hour still left in her session.

"Lottie," I said, stopping her before she got to the door, "what now?"

"I move on and forgive." She grabbed the door handle.

"Lottie, one more thing, Gil says to tell you that you belong and something about flowers. What does that mean?"

Lottie smiled softly. "Gil played the guitar and loved Tom Petty. He would always sing me the song 'Wildflowers.' Tell him that he belongs too … somewhere he feels free."

Perhaps They'll Listen

"No, I'm tired," I grumbled.

The hum of Chuck's CPAP machine was steady, so I knew it wasn't him waking me up. Connor was at school and it wasn't him, and it was rare for my dad to try and wake me, so it could only be one other thing.

I peeked one eye open to see a man, who looked to be in his late thirties. His jeans were torn and his white T-shirt and face had black marks that looked like soot. Then I smelled the smoke.

If you've ever smelled a house or building fire, you know the smell is different from any other smoky smell. I'd only had a few hours of sleep in the last few nights and I was sleep deprived and grumpy, and a midnight visitor was the last thing I was hoping to entertain.

Most of the time when I have spirit visits they simply want to tell their story, and this night was no different. So I reached over and grabbed my glasses from the nightstand and gave him a gesture to begin.

His name was Gary, and he lived in the south. Raised in a conservative home, the Bible was not just used as a guide, it was used as punishment. Gary always had feelings. He said he sensed his grandparents and had been visited by his older brother, who tragically died in a motorcycle accident when he was just eighteen. His mom and dad never swayed from their theological beliefs that seeing, hearing, feeling, or sensing the Other Side was the devil's work and nothing more.

"I knew I should've replaced the batteries in the smoke alarm." Gary shook his head, still in disbelief. "I'm just so thankful the kids and my wife were visiting her family for the night. I'm worried they will think I killed myself, though."

I looked at him, stunned. "Why would they think that?"

"I had been down. Work wasn't going well, and I was getting lazier by the day. I probably wasn't the greatest son or the greatest father, and I know that I wasn't the greatest husband. The fire, I think, started in the basement, but I promise you, I wasn't responsible."

I believed him, but I wondered why he hadn't crossed over. Why was he standing in my bedroom telling me his story? So I told him, as I tell all my visitors, that I wasn't an ambulance chaser. If I was to meet with his loved ones in the future, I would pass along his story.

He smiled a knowing smile and asked me if he could go. He thought he saw his brother in the distance and wanted to meet up with him. I wished him well, but before he left, he said, "Tell my family when you see them that perhaps they'll listen now."

I was stumped. What did that mean?

It was a week later that I received a phone call from a lady wanting to make an appointment. She was in North Carolina and had lost her husband in a house fire while she was out of town with her kids. Coincidence? I don't believe in that. I asked her if her husband's name by chance might be Gary, and I heard her gasp so I knew it was. I shared with her my encounter and ended it with what he asked of me.

"His favorite song!" she exclaimed. "He loved Don McLean's 'Starry, Starry Night.' Our last name is also McLean, and his brother would play the guitar and Gary would sing it. He always choked up when it came on the radio. It was special to him."

Maybe Gary's parents won't understand the connection, but Gary got it. I'm sure that Gary and his brother are entertaining on the Other Side. Maybe we can all learn from just that one phrase of the song because perhaps we all need to listen.

Music is an amazing way for our loved ones to deliver messages. It might be that you are feeling low or just thinking of your loved one and a song comes on the radio that reminds you of them or the lyrics have special meaning. You might wake up with a song in your head have no idea why, but it isn't as random as it seems. Look up the lyrics to see if it might be a message from the Other Side.

Chapter Fifteen

Notes from Beyond

Although there isn't mail service on the Other Side, the Other Side can surprise us with notes from beyond. You might find a forgotten note stuck in a book or a postcard from a lost love that shows up decades later, thought to be stuck in the bowels of a post office. No matter how the note shows up, it's always the right time and the right place.

Note in the Wind

Brigid was a freshman at a local university when she went missing. She was known for taking early morning jogs around campus before class, so her roommate didn't notice she was gone until that night. She promptly called Brigid's parents, who immediately contacted police. Sure enough she hadn't been to any of her classes, which was unusual with her attendance record. No return calls on her cell phone or activity on her credit or debit cards either made her parents more concerned.

After several days of searching, her parents attended a vigil and press conference, begging for someone to come forward. The crowd lit candles and prayed, but the very next day Brigid's body was found strangled not far off the jogging path. Heartbroken friends and family members gathered at the site to express their shock and grief at the sudden loss of a beautifully spirited girl. Brigid was a happy person, always giving out hugs and helping strangers. She was genuinely beautiful inside and out, and a life full of promise was snuffed out.

Hundreds came to say good-bye to Brigid. After the touching service, the guests released purple balloons, her favorite color, with handwritten notes attached.

It was just a week later when Brigid's parents were notified that the police found the murderer and that he was arrested and had confessed. The murderer had called out for help, pretending to have fallen, when he attacked her. It was just Brigid's nature to help.

It took more than two years before the guilty verdict was read. It wouldn't bring Brigid home, but her parents were grateful for closure and justice. When her mom got the mail that evening upon their return from the court house, she noticed a large manila envelope with an unfamiliar return address from clear across the country. Something told her to open it.

Dear Mr. and Mrs. Paton,

I had to write after I read the note attached to this enclosed purple balloon that I found along a nature path by my home. I was curious and looked up Brigid's information only to see the news story. I don't normally walk that path, but I did that day, and I don't believe in co-incidences. I know that this may sound strange, but I wanted to let you know that I believe I was to find that balloon and note that day to tell you that Brigid is okay. Never forget that she watches over you and she's grateful for all you've done.

Sincerely,
Lorna

Some would discount the note as coming from a crazy person, but when Brigid's mom unfolded the dirt-stained balloon and note, she saw that it was the note she, herself, had written.

Brigid—
If you can, let me know you're okay. Love you Forever
—Mom

Brigid's mom handed me the note at our session.

"I know my friends all think I'm reaching for something. Anything, but do you think…?"

Brigid's spirit stood surrounded by a beautiful and calming light, and she smiled bright.

"Death can't keep the love from her to you, or you to her. There are no coincidences and this was a beautiful sign," I confirmed.

Brigid was always reliable, and it seemed to be just the same on the Other Side.

Our loved ones love to send us objects along our path, whether a feather, coin, stone, or even balloons. They can also put it into another's path as a sign for us. Make sure to pay attention to your surroundings, as it can be easily missed.

Together Forever

My mom loved to be spoiled. It came from growing up without much. As much as she loved gifts, she loved to be romanced. Something my dad was never good at. I honestly believe my mom had unrealistic expectations from reading Harlequin novels, but she was bound and determined that my father would lavish her with gifts. It wasn't the gift, I realized later, it was the love and thought in the gift.

"Never get married on Valentine's Day, or any other holiday for that matter," she would spew. "You get gypped."

Yep, my mom and dad were married on the holiday of flowers and candy, just a few weeks short of her birthday. So my dad would try to combine it all into one gift, which didn't cut it for my mom. For forty-something years he did that, not learning his lesson or understanding why it was so important to my mother to have separate gifts.

Mom had been gone almost ten years when my dad received a brochure in the mail from a local jewelry store. It was just before Valentine's Day and on the pamphlet was a photo of a beautiful ruby pendent that had *Sally and Ron—Together Forever* etched on it. My mom and dad's names.

"See." I showed my dad. "She's still wanting her gift even from the Other Side," I teased.

My dad just shook his head, rolled his eyes, and laughed.

Love Notes from Heaven

Jordan lived in his home for twelve years when, after an exceptionally snowy winter, he discovered his roof was leaking.

"I'd never even been up in the attic," he told me, "but when I suspected we had a leak I pulled the ladder down and took a look around. Not only was there a leak, there were these." He reached into his bag and pulled out a stack of mildewed letters.

They were extra crispy and delicate, so I was afraid to even unfold them, but I knew they were special, and Jordan confirmed that.

"They are letters from a Norman to a Dora. Love letters, even. They look to be from when Norman was in the Army, possibly even away at war."

I was confused as to why he was bringing them to me, though. As if reading my mind, he asked me if I thought they were dead and if he should toss them.

"I think one of them is, Jordan. Maybe Norman. Let's see if we can track them down, though."

The computer is a wonderful and almost magical tool. It took just a few minutes and we found an active address and phone number for Norman and Dora Menard. Jordan took out his phone and dialed the number, but there wasn't an answer or an answering machine. We continued the appointment and afterward Jordan promised not to toss the letters and to try and call the number again. That same evening, Jordan told me that I was right, Norman had passed several years back but Dora was alive. He was going to meet her in a few days to give her the letters.

Jordan followed through on his promise and e-mailed me a picture of Dora holding the letters, tears streaming down her face. Norman had passed unexpectedly after a routine surgery, and Dora never got to say good-bye. When she moved, she never thought to check the attic for any belongings and forgot all about the letters.

"Norman apparently wasn't much of a talker and rarely wrote anything, except for when he was in the service. He faithfully courted Dora with beautiful notes," Jordan said. "I'm so glad that I didn't toss them and I was able to give her the love notes from Heaven."

I was glad too.

Forgotten Good-bye

"What is this, Grandma?" Emily asked, holding an envelope.

"Well, I don't know, Em. Where'd you find it?"

Emily pointed to the family Bible. "I lifted it up and this fell out."

Emily was nine years old and incredibly inquisitive, smart, and polite.

Valerie hadn't picked up the Bible for five years, since Jack died. Every morning Jack would sit at their kitchen table, cup of coffee in his one hand and a highlighter in the other, taking notes of scripture passages he loved. When Jack passed from complications of a blood clot, she shoved the Bible in the bookcase and put up a mental and emotional *Do Not Disturb* sign for God, too.

"Can I open it, Grandma?" Emily asked.

"Sure," Valerie quavered, trying not to unpack her grief all over again.

"Grandma, it's a note from Grandpa to you," Emily exclaimed. "I think you need to read this!"

Valerie trembled slightly as she took the letter.

Dear Val,

If you found this, I'm probably in Heaven. Maybe I'm no longer tone deaf and I'm even in the choir. I probably never told you I love you enough, but I do and I will forever. Never forget that. Remember that God gave us one another here, and for eternity. Psalm 55:22 says Cast thy burden upon the Lord, and He shall sustain thee: He shall never suffer the righteous to be moved. You are strong, and brave, and I love you.

Love,
Jack

It was dated the day of his passing, May 22.

He must've had a feeling, Valerie thought. *And he must've known that I'd be mad. I don't want to be frozen by anger. I need to move beyond.*

Valerie showed me the note on her second appointment with me.

"You told me that there was a good-bye, and I told you there wasn't. This was his good-bye, Kristy," she cried. "But more than a good-bye, this was his kick in the rear end that I needed."

It's so easy to become angry after a passing. I believe it to be a natural part of the grief process, and even unnatural if you aren't angry. But anger isn't a friend and can linger like someone who's overstayed their welcome. It can change you into someone you don't like. If you can work on channeling that anger into something positive where the anger doesn't saturate your love, and their memory stays alive, you will find it so much more beneficial to you and their spirit.

Ways to Channel Your Anger

- Scribble hard on paper and imagine your anger being put onto the paper and out of your system.

- Write about your anger on a piece of toilet paper and then flush it down the toilet.

- Draw, paint, color, or use another art form. Creativity is healing.

- Journal or talk to someone about your feelings. Be completely honest and don't worry about how you are perceived. Your feelings aren't wrong.

- Exercise and stay active.

- Do something in memory of your loved one.

Chapter Sixteen

Numbers

Number patterns have a vibration and deep meaning. Our loved ones on the Other Side love to show us different sequences in order to give us a message. The numbers typically have significance, such as an important event date, birth date, death date, anniversary date, high school baseball number, and so on. Not only do they show you numbers as a means to let you know that they are around but to also give you a message.

The number sequences can appear anywhere and everywhere, such as on clocks, phone numbers, license plates, receipts, mileage, price totals, and more.

What Do They Mean?

If you see a sequence of 1—it means that your loved ones are sharing a message that you are about to embark on a new beginning, and although it might be scary, they are with you.

If you see a sequence of 2—it means that your loved ones are sharing a message of "I love you" with you, and they want you to feel loved.

If you see a sequence of 3—it means that your loved ones are sharing a message that there may be a new arrival coming or a new and exciting adventure for someone in the family.

If you see a sequence of 4—it means that your loved ones are sharing a message that you've been going through a rough time and angels surround you.

If you see a sequence of 5—it means that your loved ones are sharing a message that they are concerned you feel stuck by a life circumstance, but things are about to shift. Ask them to help.

If you see a sequence of 6—it means that your loved ones are sharing a message that you are ungrounded and imbalanced and need to spend some time on self-care.

If you see a sequence of 7—it means that your loved ones are sharing a message of congratulations. You are working hard and you are about to see rewards for your perseverance.

If you see a sequence of 8—it means that your loved ones are sharing a message that there is a light at the end of the tunnel and you should be very proud of yourself. However, it is time for you to stop stalling and take steps forward.

If you see a sequence of 9—it means that your loved ones are sharing a message that you are giving of yourself too much. It is okay to say no.

If you see your birth date—the Other Side is celebrating the birth of you and reminding you that you have a purpose and are loved.

If you see a sequence of several numbers such as 4174, then you will want to add them up until you get a single digit. Example: $4+1+7+4=16$—$1+6=7$. You will then look at the meaning of 7.

You may also see sequences of death dates, anniversary dates, and birth dates of people you love, and maybe lost too. These are all Heaven nudges.

Signs by the Numbers

She didn't know how she knew, but she did. Zoe was in the shower when she felt a gust of wind that knocked the breath out of her. Her hair still soapy, she grabbed a fluffy gray towel that she and Brent had gotten as a wedding gift from his Aunt Lou. She's not sure why she thought of that—she'd never pondered the towels before—but she did as she quickly wrapped it around herself. When she heard their Siberian husky excitedly bark at the knock on the door, an odd sound because Alpine typically howled and rarely barked.

Brent's dead. She just knew it.

Still in a towel, she opened the door to see two of Brent's co-workers standing there. Not exactly coworkers, more like brothers. The police station Brent worked at since he was twenty-one years old had been a second home, and all his comrades were not just his family but her family too. And the head of the family, the Captain, was standing in front of her with tears running down his face.

"Zoe," he began, "Brent…"

Zoe slipped down on the floor and began to sob, not knowing how she'd go on. Not wanting to go on. The Captain's voice drolled on and she heard just bits and pieces.

"Ordinary traffic stop… driver had a gun… shot Brent… tried everything… announced dead at 1:17. I'm so sorry."

She wasn't even sure how she got on the couch, covered with a blanket. When she looked up at her wall clock she was stunned to see that it had stopped at 1:17. She had no idea how long she'd been sitting there, but she knew that she had to get up. It had to be about time the kids were dropped off by the bus.

The next few days were cloudy. How was she supposed to say good-bye to her soul mate? How was she supposed to raise their kids without a father? She didn't have any good answers and wasn't sure she ever would. Zoe did know that she had to be an adult, despite wanting to put the blanket over her head and pretend none of the horror existed. *First things first,* she thought, *I need to do the wash.* She looked over at the mounds of laundry strewn throughout the house. Glancing up at the kitchen clock, she was stunned to see that the clock had stopped at 1:17, Brent's death time. Grabbing her cell phone, she confirmed that the clock had indeed stopped, as it was after two o'clock. Sighing, she climbed up on a chair with new batteries in hand when Alpine began barking excitedly at the door. Quickly changing the batteries and hanging the clock back up, she jumped down and shushed Alpine, opening her front door. Expecting to see a friend or a relative, or maybe even another delivery of a casserole or flowers, she was surprised to see nobody. Alpine continued to wag his tail and turn round and round in excitement. Zoe patted Alpine on the head and closed the door to get back to her chores.

With two kids, a pile of legal paperwork to deal with, and intense grief, sleep was sparse. Her eyes finally closed and she fell into a deep sleep, only to wake up to Alpine whining, again wagging his tail.

"Alpine, really?" Zoe grabbed her cell phone off the nightstand and hit the home button to see the time: 1:17. *So odd,* she thought. Setting her phone back down, Alpine climbed into bed and fell fast asleep. "At least someone can sleep," she said out loud, bursting into tears before dozing off again.

"It's so odd, Gina," Zoe said, filling up her coffee cup with hazelnut coffee. She followed her friend to a green paisley booth and plopped down.

"Not odd at all," Gina smirked. "It's Brent trying to let you know he's around."

"I don't believe in that hogwash. Dead is dead," Zoe said, sounding brittle.

Gina looked aghast. "I disagree. Dead is alive. We are deader than they are."

"At this point, I do feel like the walking dead," Zoe laughed in response.

Gina shook her head in frustration. "Look, he's trying to give you a message. Believe me when I tell you he's going to continue this clock thing until you recognize him."

Zoe laughed again, got up and filled up her coffee mug once more. Grabbing her cell phone from her pocket, the time lit up 1:17, and she showed it to Gina.

"I don't know how much more convincing you need," Gina somberly said.

Days turned to weeks, and weeks to months. The clocks continued to malfunction and stop at 1:17 and Alpine would every once in a while run to the door, as if his master was on the porch, coming home from a long day of work. Only he wasn't and Zoe thought maybe Alpine needed a therapist.

It was just a little after the year anniversary of Brent's passing when Gina invited Zoe to a party at her house. "Nothing big, just a little get together. But, umm, don't wear jeans, wear those black slacks that make your rear end look great and that shiny top with your black cardigan."

"Oh no, this better not be a set up," Zoe said crossly.

"Uh, just a get-together. But wear those pants, okay?" Gina hung up quickly.

Zoe did as instructed, although she was far from excited, but when she got to Gina's house she realized it did feel good to be back out with the living.

"Here, I want you to meet Ethan," Gina said, grabbing Zoe's hand and dragging her over to the other part of the house. "Zoe, this is Ethan, Ethan this is Zoe. Have fun," Gina added before prancing away.

"That's not awkward at all," Zoe blushed.

Ethan was easy to talk to, though, and it was late before they realized it.

"What time is it?" Zoe asked.

"1:17," Ethan said looking at his watch. "Odd, that's my birth date."

Zoe choked on an M & M she had thrown in her mouth.

"Are you alright?" Ethan asked, obviously concerned.

Zoe immediately thought Gina put him up to this, but Ethan seemed like a stand-up guy, so she just asked him if he was pulling her leg. When he responded that he wasn't and he was confused, she explained the synchronicities.

"Maybe it's a sign," Ethan said, "from your husband."

Zoe still wasn't convinced despite the many signs, and the signs that continued as Ethan and Zoe dated. The clocks still stopped at 1:17 and it seemed every day, she would pick up her cell phone and see Brent's death time, or Ethan's birth date, however you wanted to see it. Ethan decided to turn the date into a happy one and on January 17, just as the sun set, he proposed marriage to Zoe. She said yes.

"Are you convinced yet on this whole afterlife thing?" Gina asked at Zoe's wedding reception.

Zoe nodded, laughed, and pointed to the clock. It was 1:17 a.m. She whispered her thanks to Brent for her Heaven hellos and for help in finding her a new love. Not a replacement for her passed husband, but she knew that she had to go on and live. He would want that.

The signs quieted after Ethan and Zoe said I do, but Alpine would still every so often run to the door, wagging his tail, when nobody was really there. Or at least that they could see, but maybe Alpine could.

Angels Among Us

It was a chaotic month that I am not so sure I would like to repeat. With a jury duty notice, a pending book deadline, the onset of shingles, office appointments, my husband interviewing for jobs, and trying to entertain my kids in this oppressive summer heat, I was about ready to go mad. And I had scheduled a class, the Connection to Angels, in the midst of it all. I honestly didn't have a clue what I was thinking except that I wasn't.

I raced home from my office sessions to prepare for the class. Thankfully (and gratefully) my husband had run out to the store with my shopping list for the evening and I knew that I only had to cut fruit and arrange some flowers. Right when I pulled up into my driveway I remembered that I hadn't asked him to get any bottled water. Glancing at my car's clock, it read 4:44, and all I could focus on was that I knew there wasn't a whole lot of time. I went into my garage and found a couple loose cases, carried them to the car and began counting them. I had the exact amount that I needed and sighed with relief.

A man handing out pizza coupons was walking by and I avoided any eye contact. He walked up to the car and handed me the flyer that I typically toss in the garbage without looking at. I politely thanked him, though, and he smiled and told me to have a good day. Sweat was pouring down his face and I thought of how grateful I was that my office, my car, and my home all had air conditioning.

Just as the man reached the bottom of the driveway, he said, "Ma'am, if you don't mind, could I possibly have one of those waters?"

I cringed. I was so happy to not have to run out to the store, but how could I tell this man that there was no way? "They're warm," I warned, as I tossed him the bottle.

"That's okay, Ma'am. Thank you so much!"

I smiled and nodded. Then I shut the car door and went into my cool house to tell my husband that I had to run out to the store to buy another case of water. It wasn't until I pulled out of the driveway when I realized that although he was probably just a man passing out annoying flyers, he could've been an angel. When I looked at the flyer later that night, I laughed that the pizza joint was called Angelina's Pizza, with the last three digits of the phone number 444, just like mine.

A sequence of 4s is often called angel numbers and refers to angels being around you, helping you, and reminding you of your calling. When I got my very first cell phone years back you couldn't choose your phone number like you can now, but when I saw that the last four digits were 7444, I simply laughed and knew it wasn't a coincidence.

Angels walk among us, checking up on our intentions and assisting us on our life journey. And how apropos would that be for an angel to show up at my doorstep before an angel class?

Just a few days afterward, I was still stressed to the limit with deadlines. I could still feel the tug of a shingle outbreak and tried to stay focused on my tasks at hand. My kids were volunteering at our town's library and it was their day to work. I thought it would be a perfect quiet place to sit down and write, so I grabbed my laptop to take with me. As they went to get their assignment, I sat down at a table in the back corner and began writing.

"How are you doing?" An older man with gentle eyes sat down opposite me.

I don't have time, I screamed inside, wanting to cry. "I'm okay, how are you?" I replied, clenching my jaw slightly.

"Confused," he said. "I was hoping you might be able to help me. By the way, I'm Leonard."

He went on about how he didn't have much money and he was trying to refinance his car. His son had a good job with a lot of money and he supervised his spending since his wife, his son's mom, had passed away. All he wanted to do was have enough money to take a trip to Northern Michigan or maybe visit Florida. I could see the pain of loneliness in his eyes as he spoke. He felt his independence had been stolen by his age and his son. He wanted to know how to refinance his car. I thought that was a funny question to ask a complete stranger, but, oddly enough, I knew the answer. So I told him how it typically worked and instructed him to go to his credit union or bank. Instead of leaving, he sat and chatted for another thirty minutes. I simply listened to a summary of his life story. He then got up, apologized for wasting my time, and gave me a hug and a thanks. But just as he was walking out of the library door, he stopped and turned toward me. "Kristy, do you believe in paying it forward?"

"I do, Leonard. I do," I smiled back at him.

Leonard winked and left.

Once again the idea of an angel visit crossed my mind and I grinned. It wasn't as if I thought instantly that he was an angel and I had to be on my best behavior. At first I was angry at the disruption, but it was that break that I needed to re-center myself.

I grabbed my cell phone to check the time only for it to light up 4:44. *Message received loud and clear,* I laughed.

Next time you are in a hurry or in your own world and receive an interruption—know that sometimes it might be Heaven-sent. So many people withdraw within themselves and put up walls. The hurt from the past makes it easy to do. It's easy to smile or compliment a stranger or ask an elderly neighbor if you can pick up something for them from the store, or maybe even surprise someone with an ice cream cone. You don't need wings to be an angel, just the mind-set.

8:08

It had been two months—almost to the day that Lori's mother had passed away. It was also the day before her birthday. She'd just finished what should have been a celebratory dinner with a close friend, out on the patio of a favorite restaurant, but instead she couldn't seem to kick the sadness she felt. Even the most decadent chocolate cake, with its sparkling candles, couldn't bring her out of a state she could only refer to as numb. The next day was not only her birthday, but her father's ninety-first birthday. He hadn't been well and add in the grief for his wife, she felt that the best thing to do was celebrate the day together, just in case it was the last.

As Lori said good-bye to her friend, she walked toward her car and reached for the door. There was a key fob in her purse that should have automatically unlocked it, but nothing was happening. Her friend had disappeared into a store and, despite the fact that she had a cell phone in her hand, she couldn't help but feel more alone than ever. She felt stranded and abandoned, a mirror image of her real life, but in a parking lot.

"I can't explain why, but I somehow knew it was my mother immediately. I'd been feeling since she died that she wanted me to buy a new car, and now she was going to make it a necessity rather than an option. I dumped the contents of my purse onto the hood of the car and, in tears, wondered how the key fob could have fallen out of my purse—all the while screaming at my mother that this wasn't the time to make a point," Lori told me.

After a few minutes of drama, she found the fob and finally got the door to open. As she got into the front seat, still fairly shaken, she settled into the car and reached for her phone to check for any e-mails or calls that might have been missed. It was nearly her birthday, after all. Pulling it out, she looked and 8:08 showed up on her phone—the time showing the date of her birthday and her father's.

"There's no doubt in my mind that my mother had slowed my departure from the restaurant down. She'd always made it a point to call me early in the morning, before I went to work, to be the first to say Happy Birthday. I guess this was her way of making sure I knew she intended to keep that tradition going."

The key fob never failed again.

On significant days for Lori, 8:08 continues to show up, particularly on Jewish holidays. It was the first Thanksgiving after her mother's death and the numbers kept repeating. Wherever she looked, she saw 8:08. Thanksgiving wasn't a big deal in her family and she didn't know what her mother was trying to say, but was reminded that it was also the first day of Chanukah—something that had totally slipped her mind, but clearly not her mother's.

Chapter Seventeen

All Dogs and Cats
and Even Roosters Go to Heaven

I never classified myself as a pet psychic, although people do come through on the Other Side with animals. My gift isn't speaking to animals like Doctor Doolittle, instead I communicate with the human soul who would communicate for the animal, and some of these interactions have been interesting.

I hold an annual Halloween event at an old haunted farmhouse, where I conduct a séance. The first year that I had the event I kept seeing a rooster and asked if anyone had a pet rooster, which was met by laughter, only I was serious. Nobody claimed the poor rooster, so I moved on. The next year the same rooster appeared and I again asked, was met by laughter again, and nobody claimed it. As I was getting ready for the third year's event, my husband, Chuck, told me that I needed to stop with the rooster.

"People are going to think you are crazy, Kristy. A rooster? Really?"

Chuck rarely doubted me, and my feelings were hurt. So when I saw the rooster again, I knew that it wasn't crazy, and that the rooster had a message, so I ignored Chuck's advice. Nobody claimed the poor rooster. After the event, someone came up to me who'd been to the previous two events and suggested that I was seeing a residual rooster, since we were at a farm. That made sense, but there was something about this rooster that was special. It wasn't just a rooster. The event goer's words stuck, though, and so the next day I paid a visit to the farmhouse to talk to the volunteers.

"Did the event go okay, Kristy?" one gentleman asked me.

"It went just fine, but there's something that's bothering me, and I'm wondering if one of you might be able to solve the mystery. For the past three years, I've had a rooster come through in the séance. I know it sounds weird, but do any of you know why a rooster would be so significant?"

A woman whom I had only met once before stepped forward with tears in her eyes. "A rooster, you say? Well, I think that message might be for me."

She went on to explain that she had lived on a farm and they raised all kinds of animals, but there was this one rooster that would run into the house every single night and crawl into bed with her. Her father would try to shoo it out, but the rooster was persistent and would find its way in, climb into her bed, and snuggle against her. Eventually her father stopped dissuading it from coming in. They named the rooster Pepper.

"My father passed away three years ago on Halloween, Kristy. Maybe the message wasn't just about Pepper, but my father too."

I felt relieved for figuring out the rooster mystery, and a little smug when I shared the story with Chuck. The next time I visited the farmhouse, the owner of the rooster shared photos of her and the rooster, and I just shook my head in awe. Not only do dogs and cats go to Heaven, but apparently so do roosters. I've also seen everything from horses to snakes to rabbits and so on. Why wouldn't the things we love share our heavenly home with us?

Conan the Destroyer

The white fluffy face was irresistible and although I wasn't a fan of pet shops, I went in and asked if I could hold the dog, a huge mistake because rarely do you visit with a puppy or a kitten and not want to take it home. A month beforehand my {then} husband had gone out to look for a Valentine's Day gift for me, or so he said.

"I was going to get you a Saint Bernard puppy, but, Kristy, the parents were huge and they drooled. All I could envision was Cujo from Stephen King!"

Instead, I received a stereo system that he'd had his eye on for some time. Happy Valentine's Day to me.

This puppy was a Great Pyrenees and a close relative to a Saint Bernard, without the excessive drooling. I plopped the cash down and took the male puppy home, naming him Conan, after Conan the Destroyer, a role Arnold Schwarzenegger was well-known for playing. I was often home by myself at night and thought he would make an amazing protector. But Conan wasn't a destroyer at all, even though he ended up weighing close to 150 pounds. If I had thought I was getting a guard dog, I was sadly mistaken. He thought himself a lapdog who was afraid of everything.

One day I brought home a large bag of dog food from a pet food distributor and dumped it into the garbage can that I kept in a mud room. As soon as I poured it in, Conan ran into the corner of the room and began to whine, staring intently at the can. Confused and thinking perhaps he wanted to be fed, I lifted the lid of the can only to see five small field mice staring up at me. They must've stowed away in the bag. I screamed, Conan whined, and I called my dad, who came and released the poor mice who were probably more frightened than any of us. Needless to say, Conan wouldn't eat any of that food, and I wasted more than twenty dollars. I never returned to that pet food distributor again.

I had two kids, went through a divorce, sold the family home, and moved. During all of this, Conan stayed by our side, being the gentlest and friendliest of companions to me and the kids. Upon moving, Conan began to show signs of declining, so a veterinarian appointment was made.

"I'm so sorry, but it looks as if Conan has heartworm," the doctor informed me.

"But how? I always gave him his pills!" I said, shocked.

"He's so large, and possibly your past veterinarian didn't give him a high enough dose of it."

He further explained the different treatments we could do. The treatment would require making sure he didn't move for days, and he added that it was very expensive and there were no guarantees. The kids were still quite young and I was a single mom working two jobs; I had never felt so alone in making a decision. With the promise that he wasn't in any pain, I decided to take Conan home and wait it out, not really knowing what to expect.

A few months later, I knew it was Conan's time, so I made the appointment with the doctor. He determined that Conan was going into kidney failure and informed me that it would be best to euthanize him. Holding the furry white head and reminiscing about the first time I saw him in that pet shop, I closed my eyes and sobbed. The veterinarian, who cried beside me, promised to take care of him until the end and beyond.

"You do know he goes to Heaven, right, Kristy?"

I was told all my life that animals had no souls and that they didn't go to an afterlife. I wasn't sure what to believe, but I nodded at him, thankful for his compassion and kind words.

I had called in late to work, and as I pulled into the parking lot I regretted not just taking a personal day. As I walked in, the maintenance man held the door open for me. Bart was a war veteran with a tough demeanor and a take-no-prisoners attitude. Most of the employees avoided him, almost all were afraid of him, but he was always kind to me. I usually offered him a smile and small talk, but I wasn't in the mood, so I simply nodded my thanks.

"What's wrong, Kristy?" Bart growled.

I shook my head and began to cry, choking out that I'd had to put my dog to sleep. Bart's eyes glossed over with tears, and he took my hands and held them close to his chest in a tender way.

"The unconditional love our pets give us can't ever be replaced with any human being. Know that he will always be in your heart, and I bet he will visit you as well. He will give you a sign, Kristy, I just know he will. He will show you that he's okay and that what you did was okay by him. I just know it," Bart said.

Nobody in my office knew I was working as a professional psychic medium and doing work with law enforcement on missing persons and murder cases on the weekends. Not Bart, not anybody, but it was as if I was receiving a sign of validation from an unlikely person. Bart walked with me to my office. As we made our way through the hallway, my boss, another very gruff individual, was heading toward us.

Bart held up his hand in a defensive movement, as if to tell my boss not to start anything, said, "Her dog passed away," and continued to guide me to my desk. Later that afternoon, my boss walked by and simply said, "I get it. I've been there. I'm sorry." My tears started all over again and didn't end for a few days. Telling the kids was probably the hardest thing, and each time I opened the door after work without his wagging tail welcoming me home started the waterworks all over again.

It was almost a year later when my son, Connor, called for me to come to his room. "Mom, Mom, come here and quick. Come here, Mom! Conan is here!"

Connor was probably all of five years old and I figured he was playing some game, but I went and peeked in on him. There he was, tears streaming down his face, while he petted the air. Or one would think. Connor was still in a toddler type of a bed and so if anyone with any weight sat on the bed, it sagged. Where Connor was petting, the bed sagged all the way down to the floor, yet not where Connor was sitting.

"Do you see him, Mom? Do you?"

I didn't, but I believed him.

"He has to go now," Connor said, giving Conan's spirit one more pat on the head. Then the bed bounced back into place and Connor and I simply stared in awe.

That was more than thirteen years ago, and we haven't been visited by Conan again. Although it technically wasn't my visit, it was Connor's visit, it helped me to believe that there was an afterlife for pets, and Conan was there.

Guinness

Not long after Conan's passing, we decided that it was just too hard and too sad to come home without the greeting of a dog. A friend had suggested we visit a local farm that bred Australian Shepherd puppies. I had never had an Aussie, but I read up on them and the breed seemed to be a good choice for our family.

I chose the male puppy before his eyes were even opened from a large litter of puppies. His parents were workers, because Aussies are known herders and that is what they love to do. He had freckles and was tricolored with a white lightning strike on his forehead that made the kids and me think of Harry Potter, so Potter should've been an obvious name, but Connor wanted to name him Steve. The name Steve didn't make the cut, so he became Guinness, since he was the black and tan color of the beer.

Guinney Pig, which was his nickname, didn't much like men. Being single and dating sporadically was interesting with Guinney, as he would sit at the front door, growling and not allowing any male to come into the house. It was different when I first met my {now} husband Chuck. I warned Chuck that Guinness's approval determined whether we dated or not. When Chuck and Guinness met, Guinness simply laid down by his feet. It was love at first sight for Guinness, although Guinness drove Chuck crazy with his protective barking and his sweet tooth. They were more alike than maybe Chuck wanted to admit, and ironically they shared the same birth date.

Guinness loved animals of every kind. He snuggled with our pet bunny rabbit Ginger, and he loved the cats. He wouldn't hurt a fly. He never chewed up anything or made a mess, but he did like getting into the trash and he could take a squeaker out of a toy in record time. He hated the rain and if a dog could tiptoe, he did. His favorite times were dinner and bed.

Guinness was the protector that Conan wasn't. He wasn't a fan of most men and would stand against me growling and acting as a buffer between them and me. He was also incredibly intuitive and could see my nightly visitors. If I had visits from the Other Side and he liked them, he would simply raise his head in acknowledgment and go back to sleep. If he didn't like the visitor, he would snarl until they left.

The Bells

One day, when I was still working at my corporate job, had been a rough one. The kids were with their dad, so I decided to throw the load of laundry I did that morning in the dryer and call it an early night. I thought I would read a bit before falling asleep, but the day must've taken its toll on me and before I was done with the first page of my book of choice I was fast asleep. Just a few hours later, I awoke to hearing what sounded like church bells chiming and Guinness whining and nudging my hand. Then I smelled the fire.

I ran downstairs with Guinness in tow only to see that the dryer had caught on fire while I slept. I ran back upstairs and dialed 911 and then the gas company. Within five minutes the firemen showed up. Only Guinness refused to let them in the house. He lay against me, growling.

One of the firemen bent down next to him, looked him in the eye, and said, "I'm one of the good guys." Wouldn't you know that Guinness moved over and let them in the house without a problem.

No more than fifteen minutes later, the fireman came out to inform me that all was clear.

"You're lucky that you woke up," one of the firefighters said, informing me that not only was there a fire, but there was a high level of carbon monoxide, and that they opened the windows. "What woke you up?" he inquired.

I had smoke detectors and a carbon monoxide detector and for some reason, none of them went off.

I told him that I heard bells chiming and then Guinness roused me. He nodded his head and said he'd heard of the bells many times. I gave him a crooked look.

"Angels," he simply said, patted Guinness on the head, and left.

Guinness got an extra large bone as thanks, and to this day I won't ever start the dryer if I know I'm leaving the house or going to bed.

Saying Good-bye

When Guinness reached thirteen years old, his bedtime began to get earlier and earlier. Pretty soon he was snuggling into his bed on the floor next to my side of the bed at just four in the afternoon.

It had been a tough year. My daughter was married and moved to North Carolina from Michigan and Guinness mourned her being gone. His age showed around and in his eyes. His back legs would go limp, his breathing labored, and his hearing and sight had faded. I prayed that I would just wake up to find him peacefully crossed over, but he was brave and fought. Several years before, the veterinarian diagnosed Guinness with liver cancer, but there had been no physical indication of a disease. When Micaela came home for her grandpa's funeral a month after her moving, he shook with excitement and cried. He actually cried with happiness.

Guinness wasn't a dog to me, he was like another kid. He hated me traveling and sensed when something was amiss. He was very psychic and would see the spirits that visited me, and would alert me to the ones that he didn't like. He could also sense an upcoming storm, terrorist attack, or when someone was sick, and he would chew his feet and pace to alert me. Those times he would need to be snuggled and comforted.

The night before the appointment with the veterinarian, Connor, Guinness, and I Skyped with Micaela, who was back in North Carolina, while we fed him McDonald's cheeseburgers. Guinness's hearing and sight was just about gone, but his taste buds seemed to savor his treat. Micaela said her tearful good-bye and I snuggled up with him for that entire night. First thing in the morning, I sat in the back seat with him in my lap as Chuck drove us to the vet's office. He began to jump around like a puppy, and I thought maybe I messed up. Maybe this was a huge mistake, but the evaluation showed that he was now in pain and had something neurologically wrong with him, so I made the decision to allow him to peacefully pass as he lay in my lap.

After the last injection was given, Guinness took one final breath, smiled, and was gone. The doctor nodded to me as I sobbed and held him for a bit longer, but I could feel that his soul had already crossed. We got to the car and Chuck burst into tears and held me for several minutes before we went home. Then I had to give the news to my dad, who lives with us and who adored Guinness. He informed us that a half hour before we returned all of our other animals started to howl at absolutely nothing, and so Guinness must've come to say his good-bye to his brothers and sisters.

Thirteen years with a pet was a long time. It took me awhile to get used to not having Guinness bark at the mail carrier, and even more than a year later I still sometimes forget and call him to come to bed.

A couple months after we said our good-bye to Guinness, I went to bed and found Cooper, our Siberian Husky and Guinness's best friend, laying in the spot where Guinness used to sleep, crying. We forget that animals mourn just the same. Cooper and Guinness used to compete against one another on everything, just like humans. They would bicker on everything from who would lead on their walks to who ate their food first. Guinness accepted Cooper immediately, and they were true brothers. They say elephants never forget; neither do dogs.

Keeper

Missy loved animals and had several dogs and cats that took over not only her house but also her heart. She was foster mother to any animal that came her way, from a bearded dragon to a hairless rat. When she received a phone call late one night that some kids found a newborn kitten close to death, abandoned and lying in a field, Missy didn't hesitate. With her housecoat and slippers on, she drove to the location and picked up the little orange tabby she named Keeper.

After nursing him for weeks, Keeper gained the strength and independence to play and snuggle. Rarely leaving Missy's side, he would even go into the shower with her, hardly letting his mistress out of his sight.

When Missy was battling some health issues, Keeper didn't leave her side, gently sleeping next to the body parts that ached, as if trying to heal her himself.

After fourteen short years, Keeper passed away one morning while lying in a spot of sunlight on the rocking chair that he'd claimed as his own when he was just a peanut.

"I think I feel him around me," Missy told me. "I know it probably sounds crazy."

I told her that it didn't. I don't claim to be a pet psychic, but I can see animals and I communicate with human spirits who relay messages from animals. I saw Missy's brother in spirit holding a huge orange cat that looked like the cartoon Garfield. When I told Missy, she yelped in excitement.

"My brother passed the year before Keeper. He had his problems, but he loved animals and he loved Keeper. He really has him, Kristy? You aren't just saying that?"

"I promise you," I smiled, and I continued with the message. "Your brother says that you have Keeper's ashes, along with a photo of him, on a table. He says it's like a memorial or altar for him."

Missy's eyes were bright and she nodded.

"Your brother also says that you've seen shadows and felt Keeper rub against your legs, and although you have other pets, you look down and nobody is there."

"That just happened yesterday!"

"Your brother says you would tell Keeper all the time that you'd never let anything happen to him and you shouldn't feel guilty because you loved and cared for him with all your soul."

Missy began to cry and grabbed a tissue from the box next to her, dabbing at her tears. "Maybe I should've done more."

"No, no, there isn't any more you could've done," I assured her. "Your brother also says that one day you were feeling really down and the light that is next to Keeper's ashes flashed on then off. It wasn't a short, Missy, it was Keeper letting you know that he's okay, he's being taken care of, and he wants you to be okay, too."

"Is my sadness holding him back from being at peace, Kristy?" Missy inquired.

I shook my head no. "He's in a good place and I can tell your brother loves him, too. Your loved ones, including Keeper, want you to work on finding your peace."

That love that we feel for our pets continues on the Other Side.

That Rotten Cat

Even after decades of doing readings, I am always surprised when animals come through and how they come through. One client that I'd never met before came to her session and all I could sense off her was anxiety and stress, so I started with small talk before beginning. It still didn't calm her nerves, so I decided to just ask her why she was so nervous.

"I had a horrible reading a few years ago and I'm afraid of a repeat," Lana told me.

I understood her apprehension. Readings can be damaging or rewarding, depending upon the reader. As soon as I closed my eyes, though, I saw her mom and dad come through in spirit. Her dad looked a lot like the actor and cowboy John Wayne. When I told her that she laughed and said he did, and his name was John, too. Her mom, a classy lady, stood next to her husband with a happy smile on her face. She was quieter, but a peaceful energy surrounded her. She was just happy to be with her husband.

"That's so true," Lana concurred. "She missed my dad horribly."

"Your dad says he's living on a farm on the Other Side with your mom and he's got a bunch of animals with him, including a cat."

Lana looked surprised by the cat reference. "A cat? He did, well I did too, live on a farm, so we had a lot of outdoor cats, but he was never close to any of them."

John disagreed. He went up to a screen door and opened it. Shut it. Opened it again, and then showed me a large orange tabby. He bent down and patted it on the head.

"He keeps saying you are forgetting about the rotten cat," I shared.

Lana broke out in laughter. "That would be Rotten. That's what we called the cat. He was the only one allowed in the house, and Dad would get up out of his chair, let it in and let it out and let it in again, and never once complained. Cats to us were not pets, they were mouse catchers, but Rotten was special. Oh my, I forgot all about Rotten. One day he didn't come to the door for Dad to let him in, and Dad was so distraught. He found him the next day in the woods, an animal must've gotten ahold of him. My dad never cried, and he didn't cry for Rotten either, but he was sad. I think more sad than he'd been when some of his family members passed away," she confided.

Because I Love You

I was doing a book signing when I had a brief break and was on my way to the restroom, but I felt this immense pull to my right. A middle-aged lady stood in the Romance section of the bookstore, looking at the New Release section. I could see her dad standing next to her, holding the leash of a dog in spirit.

Thinking I was just sleep deprived, I ignored it and went to the bathroom. On my way back, I ran into the same lady and again her dad was there, holding the leash of what looked like a French bulldog.

"I know this is strange," I said, feeling myself blush. "But I'm a medium and I have to let you know that your dad is on the Other Side. Although that isn't the important message, it's that he's got your dog with him."

The lady turned pale.

"I'm so sorry," I apologized and began to walk away, feeling even more embarrassed now.

The lady gently grabbed my elbow, and I turned around. "No, please, no. Can you tell what kind of dog?"

I squinted and apologized again, "I always say that I'm not a pet psychic, but I do see animals. I think it's a French bulldog."

The lady gasped and reached into her purse. At first I thought she was going to pay me, and obviously I would've refused, but instead she pulled out a picture of the exact dog I was seeing with her dad. "I had to put him to sleep yesterday. I did everything to help him, even took him to Michigan State University veterinarian school and they did surgery, but it wasn't enough."

"Your dad says that your pup had a tumor and he was in pain. You did the right thing."

The lady started to cry.

"He also said that it was the stupidest dog, but he loves you and that's why he's taking care of him."

The tears turned to boisterous laughter. "Tucker was not the brightest, and my dad never bonded with that particular dog. Oh, that's funny." Tears of laughter ran down her face. "Tell him thank you."

"You just did," I said and walked back to my signing table.

Chapter Eighteen

Lessons from Spirit

There are many reasons why someone would want to stay earth-bound instead of crossing over, such as a sudden passing, unfinished business, violent death, and fear of judgment. Or some are just content where they are. It's a choice that we have whether we cross or not, and while most do, some don't.

You can typically tell when a spirit hasn't crossed due to the anxious, nervous, or heavy energy. You don't need a medium in order to feel it either.

Years ago, I met a married couple who were my Facebook friends at a library event that I was speaking at. I'd never met them in person, and we clicked immediately. They were concerned that her father hadn't crossed over and asked if I could maybe help. I, of course, said that I would. We met first and sure enough I felt her dad, who felt trapped by circumstances here. Those circumstances were namely his very demanding and strong-willed wife, the step-mother.

"One of the last things she said to him was that he wasn't allowed to leave her, apparently he took that very seriously," they shared.

So we set up another time and we met at the cemetery where his body and gravestone were, and we crossed him over. You don't have to go to the cemetery when you do this, but that was where I was prompted to go.

The Cross Over

Helping someone cross over is more of visualization than anything, and it can happen anywhere, even a hotel room in New Orleans. Here are the steps to help them:

Protect Yourself—You want to make sure that you are speaking to a spirit of the white light (someone that is good and not a prankster). I say a prayer of protection, asking my guides and protectors to assist me by surrounding me and the spirit with loving and protective energy.

Make Sure—Make certain this is what the spirit wants. You can't force anyone to go to the Other Side. So simply ask if this is their request. If you feel a heavy feeling, that could indicate that they aren't ready, a lighter feeling is a green light. Remember that they are a person with feelings and fear too. Don't demand; have compassion. Since there is no such thing as time and space in the spirit world, the spirits can be trapped, or earthbound, for hundreds to thousands of years. Especially if I feel a heavy feeling, I will tell them what year it is and let them know that they aren't living their highest purpose by wandering. Then I check in again to see if they've changed their opinion.

Bring in Their Family—I close my eyes and visualize a brilliant white light coming down from the sky and encompassing them with love and comfort. It is a pathway of invitation. I walk with them as close to the light as I can, and I point out the souls—their family members and friends—on the Other Side, who want to help them over the threshold. If they decide not to cross, you can tell them that they are no longer welcome to be around you. Like a baby blanket to a toddler, they may feel comfortable with you and not realize that giving that up is a good thing until they realize they can't have it.

The Send Off—I offer their hand to those in the white light and visualize them crossing. If you do not see or hear anything, don't worry, simply pay attention to how you and how the energy around you feels.

Extra Help—Sometimes cross overs require a dose of extra help. I typically ask for angels and guides to assist, and will specifically call on Archangel Michael and Archangel Azrael. Michael has a blue sword that can cut ties to this earthly plane and Azrael is the angel of death and dying and provides comfort. He is often seen by twinkling yellow energy. I also ask my guides and family members on the Other Side to assist in welcoming the new soul or souls.

Final Release—I always keep the door open for a brief second and ask if any other wandering souls would like to cross over and join the party.

Close the Door—Once I feel all the spirits that decide to cross, I visualize the light dimming and the door closing. I then ask the angels to seal the doorway so nobody can cross back into this plane. I thank everyone heavenly and earthly who assisted.

Jolly

"You can call me Jolly," the spirit smiled brightly at me from the side of the bed, sitting on the windowsill that looked over the sprawling green fields.

It had only been a few hours before that my husband and two kids, Micaela and Connor, drove what felt like five miles up the dirt path to the plantation house where the moss oak greeted us. It was as if each tree stood tall with its own story to share. On either side were the old slave quarters, each one in horrible disarray.

"The slave cemetery is in back," I whispered, as if afraid to disturb the dead.

"How do you know?" Chuck slowed the car down, trying to peek around the white ruins.

A look was all that was needed to explain it.

The sun was quickly setting over the marshy lake, and we hoped to check in with still a bit of daylight to explore the grounds.

"Now watch yourself along the pathway by the lake, there are gators. The small ones are more like puppies and are just curious," the caretaker drawled. "The larger ones, well don't mess with 'em."

As if on cue, a large burp came from the nearby water.

The caretaker took us to our rooms housed in the North Guest House, turning the lanterns on to light our way. The kids took the one room with two beds, while Chuck and I took the room across the hall with the king-size bed, both were decorated in white French toile linens.

"I don't like your room, Mom," Micaela confessed. "There's something about it that feels … heavy." Micaela was sensitive, just as her brother, Connor, was. While Connor embraced the gift, Micaela was less than thrilled with mine and even more so with her own.

I took a few deep breaths and psychically checked out both rooms only to get an all clear from my guides.

Chuck and I unpacked as the kids explored, flashlights in hand. It wasn't long before they ventured back and we decided we were more hungry than curious. We trekked back down the long path to the main road to hunt for pizza.

A full belly, a hot shower, and a comfortable bed was convincing me to call it an early night. It couldn't have been ten minutes after shutting my eyes when a spirit, who introduced himself as Jolly, showed up for a visit. He wasn't the least bit surprised that I could see him or that I was even there. It was as if he was even expecting us. Apparently my guides were on vacation too, for not picking up on the visitor.

"Can I help you cross over? Is there something you need my help on?" I asked him, stuttering a bit.

"No, Ma'am."

I looked at him, confused. Jolly threw his head back and laughed the deepest laugh I'd ever heard. I looked over at my husband, who incredibly was still sleeping soundly.

"Did you work here?" I asked, already knowing the answer, but I wasn't quite sure what was happening. I was tired and really just wanted to get to the bottom of the visit.

"I did, Ma'am. I was the leader here for many, many years. This was my home."

I sat up on my pillow and looked at him. "Home? You were enslaved, right? Was it horrible?"

"It was all I knew. All we knew. I hold no ill regrets."

"So why are you still here?" I asked, still confused.

"Because it's home and I'm still the caretaker," Jolly explained.

"Isn't it time to find peace?"

"I'm at peace, but I'm afraid that the world isn't."

"What about justice? What about that?" I asked.

"Seeking justice creates more sin. Peace creates more peace."

I sighed with understanding. I realized he was speaking of something completely different than I was, but it seemed to be eerily related to current events.

"Peace," Jolly began. "Peace happens when you forgive, whether deserved or not. Most of all, peace happens when you realize you deserve peace."

Jolly and I spoke for some time, along with another lady he introduced as Franny. The next morning my family and I went to the slave cemetery and paid our respects. Jolly simply nodded a hello to me, with a big jolly smile on his face in thanks.

I couldn't help but think that if someone who was enslaved for decades could go into the afterlife with peace, well, I could only hope for our souls today.

Naked and Not Afraid

One of the constant things that spirit tells me on the Other Side is that they are still the same person they were in life, only they are able to look over their earthly experiences and learn from them.

I was doing a gallery reading several years back at an old and haunted paper mill. Not only were the ticket holders' loved ones from the Other Side gathered around for me to share their messages, but so were the spirits of the mill and the surrounding town. If ever I felt on display, it was that afternoon.

Trying to separate the spirits so I could give clear and concise messages, I noticed one spirit in the back of the room—naked. One of the questions I frequently get is how can spirits wear clothes? Well, they don't really, but because we are physical beings, we see them how we remember them, the way their hair color and style was, their eye color, their size and shape, and the clothes they frequently wore. This one man in spirit, however, was in his birthday suit and strutting around like Mick Jagger on stage. I checked in with my guides to see if he was someone from the town, but they told me that he had a message for someone sitting in the audience.

Oh boy, I hoped someone connected to this man. I hemmed and hawed for a few moments and decided to just say it like it was.

"I have a naked man with a bushy beard and a huge and mischievous smile on his face. He died from a massive heart attack. I think his name starts with an *H* and he loves to strut around to good old-fashioned rock and roll. He's now singing Bob Seger," I winced, embarrassed to look at the naked spirit, and just as embarrassed to look at the crowd. A gasp made me peer over to one table where a couple sat blushing.

The woman nodded her head. "Yes, that would be Uncle Harold. He was the odd one in the family, and at every gathering he would strip down completely naked and start dancing. I can't believe he is here."

I couldn't believe he was here either, and I couldn't believe that someone claimed him.

"Harold, put on some clothes and tell me why you're here," the woman's husband growled.

Instead of listening, Harold continued to dance around like a hippie at Woodstock. I moved on to another spirit, but Harold interrupted me and apologized. "Tell Maria that her mom always loved me for me, and I will be there as she makes her transition. I'll even wear clothes." Harold began spinning around again as I passed along the message.

"My mom has days left on this Earth. Harold wasn't just her brother, he was also her best friend, despite Harold's issues. That's reassuring to know," she confirmed.

Thankfully, Harold has been my only *male* naked spirit, but it solidified that we don't change on the Other Side. If Harold loved being naked here, he's going to be naked there.

There have been several reports of naked spirits, though, and I found that it wasn't as unusual as it may seem. Alice Mabel Gray was a writer and mathematician who resided in Indiana. She was nicknamed Diana of the Dunes, and she lived in a remote cabin outside of the main town. Because of the seclusion, she would often skinny dip in Lake Michigan. When she passed away in 1925, her ashes were scattered along the dunes, but there have been many people who've seen the spirit of a naked lady coming out of Lake Michigan during the summer full moons.

NOLA

In November 2015, my husband and I took a long weekend to Louisiana, with our first stop in New Orleans. I had been trying to convince him to go for years, but he was always apprehensive, seeing as so much death and sadness had occurred in the city that he thought it would be overwhelming for me. He wasn't the only one who was skeptical of the trip.

"Don't people get killed there?" one friend asked me.

"People die everywhere," I responded with a laugh.

I knew that wasn't what she meant, but hey, I was from Detroit after all, and crime smart.

Immediately after getting off the plane I could feel the shift in energy. It wasn't as intense as I'd feared, thankfully, but the air felt electric and alive. We got our rental car and just as we got on the freeway heading to the French Quarter, warning signs began to light up on the dash.

"I think we have an almost flat tire and who knows what else," Chuck shared, with a hint of panic in his voice. "There's absolutely nowhere to stop."

There was bumper to bumper traffic and the Superdome ahead of us without any exits and no gas stations in sight.

Chuck's nervousness was making me nervous, and I just wanted to turn around and get back on the plane for home. *Maybe he was right. Maybe I should've listened to him,* I thought, apologizing to him in my head. Before I could make my suggestion, our GPS alerted us that the next exit was ours and we saw a gas station on the corner.

"Just remember not to stop anyplace that is dark," another friend who'd traveled to New Orleans warned us.

"Really? Do you think we are dumb?" I'd replied.

The sun had set and although there were street lights and lights underneath the gas pumps, the air hose was in a dark alleyway, and I thought the joke was on us. Neither of us had change for the machine, so Chuck had to run into the station, past a crowd of prostitutes and their pimps, who were having a meeting. Without an air gauge or a light, Chuck fumbled around and quickly added air to the tires. Before we knew it, we were on our way to the hotel, unscathed.

Ironically, our hotel was just a couple blocks away. Now you would think I would've tried to choose the least haunted hotel so as to get some sleep, and that is exactly what I thought I had done. That is until I was reading a travel book on the plane only to discover that I had chosen the *most* haunted hotel in the French Quarter. Chuck was thrilled and thought I'd done it on purpose.

"I'll sleep fine," he smugly touted. "It's you who will have the problem!"

He was right, but I had this covered. Something told me to bring sage and a whole lot of crystals to wear—enough that they would make Mr. T from the A-Team jealous.

Ghost sightings and hauntings are nothing new to New Orleans and the French Quarter. It was apparently very common at the Dauphine Orleans Hotel, where we were staying. A room right next to the bar once served as May Baily's infamous red light district known as Storyville. They offered a variety of spirits from Civil War soldiers to their well-dressed ladies-of-the-evening.

Chuck was intrigued. These wouldn't just be any spirits, they would be *interesting* spirits.

We were culture shocked after venturing out and losing our way onto Bourbon Street, the iconic street filled with music, booze, street performers, and pickpockets. We decided to grab some carryout and call it an early night. From our room we could hear the shouts, the gunfire, and the music. Chuck grabbed his ear plugs and kissed me goodnight. I lay down in the bed, staring at the cathedral ceilings of the cottage room.

The red light next to May Baily's bar danced shadows along the white walls. A shadow passed by the room, which I thought was odd seeing as we had the last room, and then it walked toward the bar. I tried to pretend that it was simply a shadow from someone below, but after seeing the shadow again, I quietly got out of bed and looked outside only to see nobody in the courtyard, even the bar looked dark and locked up. I turned around to see Chuck fast asleep and next to my side of the bed stood the spirit of a naked female. I think I startled her as much as she did me, and she disappeared. There wasn't another visit that evening, but sleep was fitful.

The next day, we sat at the bar at May Baily's, chatting up the bartender. "Do you have any reports of naked women in spirit?" I inquired.

The bartender nodded, set her dishrag down, and asked me to tell my experience.

"That was probably Julia," she said.

Julia was said to live in the 1800s, and, according to legend, was a beautiful lady with slave roots, but she was fair skinned. She was a commodity in the area and her lover told her he would only marry her if she proved her love. Not by being faithful, but by spending a night naked on the roof of what some believe to be a building on Royal Street, just a couple blocks from where we were staying. Julia was desperate to be loved and to have stability in her life, a roof over her head, and a warm bed underneath her, so a night on the roof was nothing. It was a cold and damp December night when she climbed onto the roof and laid down on the slippery peek while naked. The next morning, she was found dead.

Was it the elements that killed her on that lonely rooftop in the stark night, or was it someone who couldn't believe she went through with the dare and didn't want to pay up?

The next evening, Chuck and I felt a bit more accustomed to the area, especially after some day tours. We had a delicious dinner of po'boys and dirty rice and spent some time watching the street performers before going back to the hotel and sitting poolside, talking to other guests, sharing adventures, politics, and ghost stories. I finally couldn't keep my eyes open and so we said our goodbyes and headed upstairs to our room. I saw the bartender exit the bar and lock up the door and the gate. I thought it was odd, since it was still early on a Friday night, but before I could ponder it further I fell into a deep slumber. Then I was awoken by Julia.

"Do you need my help in crossing over?" I asked her, looking over at Chuck who was fast asleep.

She quietly nodded.

"Is there more to your story than what they tell?"

She nodded again.

"Do you want to share?"

Julia shook her head no and began to cry. I wasn't about to press her; I was there to help her.

"You've got loved ones on the Other Side that I'm sure miss you. Are you ready?"

Julia took my hand in hers and I began the cross over. Within minutes, I felt her energy leave. A deep peace came over the room and I snuggled back down into the bed and fell asleep.

Chapter Nineteen

Spirit Connection

Electronics are easy for loved ones on the Other Side to manipulate to let you know they are around. Some ways they can utilize electronics are:

- Computers will malfunction
- Phones will ring
- Street lights will turn on or off, or flash repeatedly
- Alarm clocks can go off when they aren't set or be set for a poignant time
- Lights may flicker, turn off or on
- Children's toys can be played with
- Doorbells will ring
- Light bulbs burn out or flash
- Smoke alarms will sound when there is no emergency
- Televisions and radios will be changed, turned off, turned on, or simply stop working

Eve

One Christmas Eve, a little girl with a big but damaged heart took her last breath on this Earth. Incidentally, her name was Eve. She was only seven years old with the wisdom of a ninety-seven-year-old. Her mom called her bossy and demanding from her first cry, and she wasn't surprised when Eve demanded that her mom, dad, sister, and brother sit at her bedside so that she could say her goodbye; her breathing labored and her soul tired.

"I'm not going to be here tomorrow." Eve's pretty blue eyes closed, and she clenched her fists as if fighting off the pain. "But Santa will still come and I want you to still celebrate Christmas. I want you to open your stockings and eat cookies and play games, and go to Grandma's house for dinner, and do all the things we always did. Nothing changes except me not being there. I will be on my trip to Heaven, but I will let you know when I get there."

Neither Eve's mom nor dad wanted to think of the next hour. The next day. Or the day after that. Or after that. Eve was persistent that Christmas not be ruined because of her. And just as Eve lived her short seven years with determination, she passed away with the same grit—at 11:58 p.m. on Christmas Eve as her family sang Christmas songs around her stuffed animal–covered hospital bed.

Eve's mom set her alarm clock so she could get the presents around the tree before the other two got up, all the while knowing she wouldn't need it because there'd be no sleep. The house felt different without her Eve, and would never be the same afterward, but she'd made a promise that they would have Christmas. Staring at the tree lights through her tears, she saw the star at the top blink off and then on. *Must be a short in the wire,* she thought. She laid on the couch and closed her eyes only to be awoken by an ornament that played music if you pushed the button. Only nobody was there to push the button. And then the star blinked on and off again. Eve was letting her know she made it. It had to be. Eve's mom took the blanket that had been wrapped around her daughter in the hospital and hugged it close. No, it wouldn't be the same, but nothing ever was, with or without adversities.

"We'll never forget you, Eve," she whispered.

And the star blinked off and then on again and Eve's mom smiled.

It's easy to not move forward after a loss, but in order to progress we must put one foot in front of the next and walk through the hurt, remember the happy, and find the present. Without forward movement in life, we get stuck in depression and sadness. The past is just that. It's okay to be angry and stomp. Feeling is the beginning of healing. Letting go of the sorrow isn't about forgetting, it is allowing our loved ones to travel; to take their journey, and yet what we sometimes forget is that they come back to us.

Include your loved ones on the Other Side in on your special festivities. In a quiet, comfortable place, sit near a picture of them. Have a conversation with them, telling them about your days and saying everything you need or desire to say. Remember the sound of their voice, how they spoke, their favorite words and imagine what they might say back to you. Listen. Burn a candle that reminds you of their favorite scent. Bake their favorite cookie. Holidays, anniversaries, birthdays, and special celebrations have a way of opening up the scars that you thought had healed, but our loved ones want us to not live in the past, but include them in our present. That in itself is the best gift we can give ourselves, and them too.

Eve's mom told me that they bought a new star this year for their tree. This one goes off and on too. Eve's determination and strong will remains constant, even in the afterlife.

Ashes to Ashes

I rarely do psychic parties, but here I was sitting in a bedroom squished between a bed and a closet with a small table in between two chairs. The host and homeowner sat down across from me after I had already completed readings for a dozen of her guests. She looked tired, and I wondered if this reading would go well. When people aren't open to receiving, whether from skepticism, health issues, or exhaustion, the connection to the Other Side could be fuzzy. Fortunately, as soon as I closed my eyes her dad came through.

"Your dad is standing right there, Margie," I pointed by the closet door, "and he wants to know why his ashes are here and not buried like he requested." I opened my eyes and looked at her curiously.

Margie sighed and then laughed. She reached over and swung open the closet door, pointing to a large wooden box sitting on the top shelf.

"That's Dad's ashes?" I asked, surprised.

Margie nodded. "Yep, that's Dad right there. The family is squabbling over where he is supposed to go and then squabbling over the money to put him here or there, so for the past five years he's been in my closet."

The lights flickered a few times, but stayed on. Margie and I both looked at one another in awe.

"Has he been doing that often?" I asked.

Margie laughed. "Oh, so that's Dad, huh? Light bulbs burn out constantly, and I've even had an electrician out who said nothing was wrong."

"Yep, he's not happy that his wishes were ignored."

Margie's dad stood there, his face an angry red. I was waiting for the whole box of ashes to fall and scatter everywhere. Instead, he took a deep breath and told me to tell her that she knew his wishes and disappeared.

"I will talk to the family again and get it settled," Margie promised. "Does it really matter where his ashes are, though?"

It is a question I am often asked. If they're dead then why do they care if they are ashes or in a coffin, sprinkled on a golf course or in a lake? It's a tricky question and there isn't a one-size-fits-all because it depends upon the person. In Margie's dad's case, he told them he wanted to be buried with his wife, who passed several years before. He didn't want to be scattered, but buried, and that cost money the family wasn't happy about putting out, despite his wishes and his life insurance policy he left to them. It wasn't the matter of where his ashes were exactly, but that his wishes were fulfilled, and they weren't.

If there wasn't a discussion about burial and there's a question, you know your loved one and you know what they'd want even if it wasn't discussed. Go with your gut. Use your instinct. I'm sure Margie's intuition wasn't telling her to leave Dad in the closet.

The Haunted Television

Christmas Eve in our family is the day we celebrate Christmas. When my mom passed away, I inherited hosting the holiday. The family gathered for food, dessert, and gifts. It had been a tradition before I was born and typically took place at the grandparents' house. Me and my family lived with my dad in his house, so technically I was living in the grandparents' house, and I was in charge of the festivities.

When my mom passed away, my dad received life insurance money. With his love for electronics, especially television sets, he soon headed to a big box store to buy himself a large television set.

"Mom's going to haunt you and that television set," I told Dad.

"Yeah, well, she was always mad at me, so that wouldn't be anything new," he replied.

All I could do was shake my head, half in humor and half in disgust. My dad was a lot like a little boy, and without my mom's sound voice, I was worried I'd have to be the responsible party.

Dad brought the television home and put it in his basement apartment. Immediately there were issues. Countless repair men came in and out of the house until finally my dad had enough and told me to put the television in my family room. He was going to buy another.

"Oh no, I don't want Mom upset with me," I told my dad, who just rolled his eyes at me.

Sure enough, though, my dad went out and bought the latest and greatest television. My husband put the haunted television in our family room.

"Look, Mom, this wasn't my idea," I said as Chuck hooked up the cable to it.

Chuck just laughed in agreement with me.

That Christmas, as we all sat around eating and exchanging gifts, we had the television on a station that was playing Christmas music. Only an hour into the party, the television made a huge boom, sparked flames in back of it, and went out.

My dad looked at me in shock. All I could respond with was, "Mom just wants to say hi."

The television was toast. Mom absolutely showed us all who was still boss. She didn't approve of the purchase from the Other Side.

Chapter Twenty

Mistaken Identity

St. Augustine, Florida, was calling to me, and I wasn't sure why. A friend lived there years ago and she always shared her tales of how beautiful it was. Although it was beautiful and the nation's oldest city, there was nothing that really resonated as to why I had to visit. Thankfully, my husband has been through this with me endless times—trips planned without any details as to why we were heading where we were heading—and this trip was no different.

So on a cold February day, Chuck and I boarded a plane to Orlando. We drove almost two hours to the Atlantic coast of Florida to St. Augustine, a town named in honor of the patron saint (on whose feast day the Spanish had sighted shore).

The sun shone through the breaking clouds, casting lights off the harbor. We lazily walked the cobblestone streets, taking in the Spanish architecture. Archways led to more shops, some hidden well, and it was like a city within a city. Tourists chatted in an array of languages, all seemingly enamored with the history and preserved culture that echoed around us. Chuck ran into a store to look at a shirt and, seeing as my feet were aching, I waited on a bench, enjoying the warm wind.

It was soon after I took a seat in that alleyway surrounded with begonias when I noticed a lady staring at me. Now, I tend to do fun styles and colors with my hair and that month I had purple highlights, so it wasn't peculiar to find someone giving me an odd look, but as she continued to stare, she also stepped toward me. I smiled politely and looked down at my phone, all the while still feeling her looking at me. Now curious, I glanced back up to find her standing in front of me.

"Sesha?"

"Excuse me?" I answered.

"I'm so sorry," the lady apologized. "You look just like my best friend—" She stopped mid-sentence and started to walk quickly away.

"No, please, don't go," I called out to her, standing up. "I look like a friend of yours who's passed away?"

The lady whipped back around. Her coloring had changed to a pale white.

"Yes, you look like Sesha. She died last year from cancer. I can't believe how much you look like her!" Tears began to drop down her cheek onto the uneven brick sidewalk.

Unsure of what to do or say, I muttered, "I'm so sorry for your loss."

"I didn't get to say good-bye to her and when I saw you …! Oh my goodness do you look like her!" The lady continued to take in every wrinkle and line in my face.

I could see Chuck at the counter with his purchase and wondered what to do with this lady who was enamored that I was her best friend's doppelgänger.

"You know, I believe that we are given signs from our loved ones all the time and we sometimes don't recognize them. Maybe you seeing me is your friend's way of letting you know to stop feeling guilty about not saying good-bye. In fact, I bet she didn't want a good-bye at all. You probably never even said good-bye when you spoke on the phone or when leaving her house. You probably said something like 'later' and 'I love you', right?"

"Wait, how did you know that?"

"Lucky guess," I smiled.

Standing in back of the lady was the spirit of a radiant redhead. The spirit nodded at me and made a motion of rocking a baby and pointed to the pink flowers planted next to me.

Sometimes communicating with spirits was like charades. In order to pick up on any small nuances, I have to pick up on the clues they give me.

"Plus, I think her spirit lives on in your new granddaughter. There's no good-bye, just a lot of hellos."

"How did you …?"

"Lucky guess," I repeated.

"My daughter had a baby girl in November, and she gave her my friend's middle name," the woman explained, her eyes still wide in awe.

Chuck motioned that he was done, unaware that I was giving a message, but I thought it best to leave her with that anyhow. I simply waved good-bye and walked away, grabbing Chuck's hand and walking down the street without looking back.

"What was that all about?" Chuck asked me.

"A sign. A sign for that lady." I thought pensively and added, "And a sign for me, too."

Before I could explain further, our trolley pulled up and we had to make a mad dash to catch it. As the trolley driver pointed out historical locations, giving us lore, legends, and historical facts, I thought back to the lady in the alleyway. It wasn't the fact that I looked like her friend that had me pondering the synchronicities of signs, it was the name.

Long ago I had a reading with a medium who told me that I was guided by a woman with red hair who died on my birthday. "Did I know this lady?" I asked the medium at the time. He said I did, but you would think that I would remember someone who died on my birthday, right? It wasn't until a couple weeks later while I was driving and daydreaming when I recalled who it was. A close friend of the family had passed away years previously from cancer, on my birth date. She was a spirited woman who liked to argue and prove her point with everything from politics to the weather. Everyone blamed the red hair for her extra hot temper, but she would help anyone and everyone despite her brassy personality. I would think of her here and there, but not as often as I probably should have. Her name was Sesha and she was originally from Florida. So, even though I was able to give a complete stranger a message, she did so for me in return as well.

Have you ever sat at a stoplight and glanced to the side only to see someone who looked like your grandpa, who had passed away years before? Or met someone who had the same mannerisms as your mom, who you've been missing since her earthly departure? The so-called random occurrences are far from being random and are the Heaven hellos. Most don't have any earth-shattering meaning. It's just like when you call your friend and have nothing really to talk about, you just feel the need to make the connection. Those on the Other Side do the same thing in the signs and symbols that they show us.

Chapter Twenty-One

Calls from the Other Side

Oftentimes the call will come through normal, but the connection is often bad. The voice is recognizable, but may sound faint. The call doesn't last long, whether the receiver hung up in shock or the message is passed along and the call is terminated.

Afternoon Checkup

It was a fluke that they even found the cancer. Cheryl hadn't been feeling well for weeks. She was a dependable employee and rarely even called in to work. Her boss could see that not only was Cheryl looking worse for the wear, her work was suffering as well. Cheryl's typical light step and bright smile was replaced with dark circles and countless yawns. Concerned for her, Cheryl's boss urged her to go to the doctor.

"You're probably anemic. Or maybe it's your thyroid. Whatever it is isn't going away, and I'd like you to take tomorrow off to try and figure out what it is," Cheryl's boss told her on a Tuesday afternoon.

Cheryl was embarrassed. She'd been a dedicated employee and every evaluation had been stellar, but now her boss was forcing her to go to the doctor. She did what she was told and called for an appointment for the next morning. It wasn't that Cheryl didn't like to go to the doctor, it was that she was never sick.

"Mom, I'm sure I'm fine," she told her mom that afternoon on the phone. "It's probably just a bug."

Her mom expressed worry and had her promise that she'd call her as soon as she was out of the doctor's office.

Cheryl was not just dependable with work, she was a faithful friend and daughter, too. After her dad passed, she made it a habit of calling her mom every single day at four in the afternoon to just check in. The conversations never lasted long, but it was something she looked forward to, and something her mom loved too. It was their afternoon checkup.

The next morning she woke up feeling even worse than before. Although she wouldn't say she was grateful for a doctor's appointment, she was hoping for quick fix and then back to her everyday life that she was content with.

She knew immediately that there wouldn't be a quick fix when she saw her doctor's face.

"We have to run tests, Cheryl," Dr. Luvix said. "But I don't like your symptoms, and I really don't like this lump I'm feeling in your abdomen. We'll draw blood, and I'll call you this evening."

"This evening?" Cheryl exclaimed. "Doesn't it take a week to get blood back?"

Dr. Luvix gave Cheryl an uneasy look and no words needed to be shared.

It was just a couple hours later when Cheryl received the phone call and was told to immediately get to the hospital for tests and possible surgery in the morning. They were pretty certain she had ovarian cancer.

After calling her mom and her boss, she packed a bag for the hospital. It was a surreal moment as she pulled into the hospital lot and walked up to registration. Afterward, the days blended into months with treatment for ovarian, cervical, and colon cancer. With her mom and her sister by her side, she fought a hard fight. But just six months after being diagnosed, Cheryl passed away with her family by her side.

Cheryl's mom, Lydia, was devastated. Although she still had her other daughter, whom she adored and loved, Cheryl was the one who checked up on her. She knew she'd miss that about her every day. And for the first week when four o'clock struck on her mom's Grandfather clock, she'd tell Cheryl that she was missing her.

A week afterward, though, something unusual happened— Lydia's phone rang at four o'clock in the afternoon. She'd answer it, but nobody replied. All she could hear was various background noises like someone was at a cocktail party or at a restaurant. She thought it was peculiar, but even more strange when it happened every single day at four o'clock for two weeks straight. That's when she contacted me.

"Is someone playing a trick on me, Kristy? If they are, well, how mean is that?" Lydia inquired.

It wasn't a trick, though. Calls from beyond were actually quite common as a means for those on the Other Side to communicate. It doesn't mean that Heaven has a pay phone, but phones are electronic devices and are easily manipulated as a form of communication.

Seeing as four o'clock was significant to Cheryl and Lydia, it only made sense that Cheryl was staying dependable on the Other Side, just as she was in the physical world.

"I want her to enjoy her Heaven, Kristy. I want her to be okay. To be honest, the calls creep me out a bit."

"Next time you receive a phone call, tell her that. Tell her that you appreciate the phone calls, but you will be alright and you want her to be at peace."

Lydia nodded in agreement and then began to cry. Even though she did want Cheryl to be at peace, the calls, although confusing, were also reassuring.

A week later, Lydia checked in with me. She let me know that on the day we talked she received another call and she did what I recommended.

"I haven't received another call from her since, but I asked her on the last call that she send me another sign like a feather. Wouldn't you know that I woke up this morning, washed my face, and right there on the bathroom counter was a large white feather."

The purpose of calls is typically a farewell, but there have been documents of mysterious calls that offered warnings on impending danger. Phone calls typically happen during holidays, on birth dates, and other meaningful times. They can occur on a landline or a cell phone just the same.

The Final Love

I had one client who called her son because she was concerned he was late coming home. He answered and apologized for not being home on time, offering the explanation that traffic was bad and there was an accident. She told him to be careful and said she loved him, and he responded that he loved her, too.

An hour later, she received a call that her son had died instantly in a horrible traffic accident a half hour before she placed the phone call. She thought the time was wrong and it was a huge mistake. For days she thought maybe her call to him aided in the accident. She always told him never to answer the phone while he was driving, but phone records confirmed that the call took place after his death. It was his final I love you.

A Doctor Here and a Doctor There

Shelly loved the house as soon as she pulled in to the driveway. It was a small Cape Cod–style home, and everything she'd envisioned for her small family. There was a warmth about it that called to her and she knew it was perfect, and her husband agreed.

A couple months later, they were moving in. Her husband had been called out of town on business, and so she was alone with their eight-month-old son, Alex. Between feedings and the work that babies conjure, Shelly dusted and sparkled up the rustic hardwood floors. As soon as Alex went down for his afternoon nap, she snuck out to the front gardens and cut some forsythia and pussy willows to add to her dining room table. She couldn't help but feel so grateful for her country home.

When she went back into the home, she heard Alex crying. *That's odd,* she thought. He was typically a great napper. As she neared his crib, she saw that his face was red and splotchy with tears. "What's wrong, Bud? Did you have a nightmare?" Shelly lifted him up and took note that he felt warm. Thinking it was just from his tantrum, she carried him to the kitchen to fix him some lunch, but he would have none of it. For the rest of the day, he was especially clingy and snuggled on her chest as she watched television.

Deciding to call it an early night, she carefully carried Alex to his nursery and placed him in his crib, giving him a kiss on the forehead. He still felt a bit warm, she thought, and decided to call the doctor in the morning if he was still under the weather.

She disliked her husband being away, but having the bed to herself was a luxury, and so Shelly placed herself in the middle of the king-size bed with a romance novel. Maybe a half hour after retiring, her cell phone rang. Anticipating her husband calling to check up on her, she was surprised to see that the caller identification was noted by eight zeros. Although she typically didn't answer no number calls, something made her do it anyhow.

"Hello?" she said into the receiver.

"You need to check on the baby," a male voice responded.

"Excuse me?" she asked, confused. "Who is this?"

"The baby. You need to check on the baby now!"

The phone went dead. Shaken, she got off the bed and ran to Alex's room with the cell phone still in her hand. She could hear odd gurgles and snapped on the overhead light. She saw Alex having a seizure.

"911, what is your emergency?"

"My son is under a year and he's having a seizure," she replied, stunned.

It was just a matter of a few minutes before the ambulance came and they were whisked away to the hospital.

The attending doctor assured Shelly that Alex would be okay, but he was diagnosed with the early symptoms of meningitis and would have to stay in the hospital for treatments for about a week or more.

"It's a good thing that you caught it when you did or else I'm not sure what the prognosis would be," the doctor shared.

Shelly thanked the doctor, but she knew that it wasn't her who saved Alex's life, it was the strange man on the phone. When her husband finally got to the hospital, she told him everything that happened.

"That can't be," he smirked. "A mysterious caller told you to check on Alex? Were you dreaming, maybe?"

Shelly shook her head and showed him the number and time on her history, but it was met with a simple shrug.

Almost two weeks later, she was able to bring Alex home. She was met in the driveway by a neighbor. They'd hardly been there before the incident happened and they just weren't home to socialize.

The neighbor introduced herself as Nora. She was in her late sixties with short brown hair and beautiful blue eyes, and she held out a tray for Shelly. "I made you some muffins. I'd hoped to catch you a few times, but you must have a busy schedule."

Shelly introduced her family and shared that Alex had been in the hospital.

"Nora, have you lived around here long? Do you know who lived in the house before we moved in?"

Nora gave Shelly a strange look before answering. "I have and I do. The home was originally built by Dr. Whittier around 1930, and it was kept in the family until Dr. Whittier's widow passed away."

"You said he was a doctor?" Shelly choked.

"Yes, a pediatrician."

Although Shelly couldn't verify that it was Dr. Whittier who saved Alex's life, she was incredibly thankful and credited him for the phone call, despite her skeptical husband.

It's a Boy

"Grandma, you have to stick with us. I'm getting married next week. Please don't die," Chloe begged her ailing grandmother.

She didn't want to sound selfish, but the timing was horrible. Most of all she wanted her grandma at the wedding. Chloe had been what many refer to as an old soul, and all the while growing up instead of hanging out with kids her age, she would go over to her grandma's house, drink tea, and chat. Grandma Stella taught her how to tend properly to roses and how to set a formal dining table. Grandma Stella was her favorite person in the whole world, and she wasn't ready to let her go. She knew it was selfish, but it was the truth.

Her grandma grabbed Chloe's hand and gently patted it. "I will always be with you," she reassured Chloe, before taking her last breath.

Chloe knew that her grandma was with her grandpa and was happy for that, but she didn't know how to get married and grieve at the same time. Her family reassured her that her grandmother wouldn't want her to be sad and would want the wedding to go on, and so a small funeral was held the very next day.

Standing next to the gravesite, Chloe asked her grandma to keep her promise. "I still need you, Grandma."

The wedding was beautiful, and Chloe had decided to put together a small memorial of the loved ones they had lost on both sides of the family. Next to her grandma's photo, she set a wilted rose from her funeral bouquet. Kissing her grandma's photo, she made her way down the aisle to her new married life.

It was almost a year to the date of her grandma's passing when her landline rang. She thought it was odd, since she rarely used it, but she answered it. Before she could say hello, a familiar voice chimed in on the other end.

"It's a boy, Chlo."

And then the phone went dead.

Chlo—only her grandma called her that. She gasped. It did sound like her grandma, she thought, but how odd.

During our session on a warm Michigan summer evening a week later, I told her, "Yep, in fact I think you'll get pregnant in the next couple weeks." I smiled.

"The doctors have all told me I'll never have a child. Never. Now you are saying you see a baby in the next year? Really?"

Her and her husband had tried to get pregnant. They saw the best fertility doctors and did expensive treatments, but nothing. Her grandma was bound and determined to give her grandaughter a gift.

I could see three sparkles, souls, that she had already miscarried. I knew she was hurting, but her grandma held a child in her arms and I knew it would be okay.

A week after her heavenly phone call and her appointment with me, she started to feel as if she were coming down with the flu.

"Maybe you should take a pregnancy test," her husband teased.

But he was right, Chloe was pregnant. Her twenty-week ultrasound confirmed that they were expecting a baby boy. Twenty weeks later, the new parents held their baby.

I hadn't heard from the couple, which wasn't at all abnormal, but out of the blue on a wintry February morning I received a text message with the picture of a beautiful baby boy.

"We named him Christopher—in honor of you, Kristy," she wrote.

To say that I sobbed would be an understatement. I take no credit. I'm just a messenger. Besides that, we are all given the gift of believing. Believing in the impossible. Believing in ourselves. Believing that everything will be okay. Chloe simply said she let go, had faith, and believed. And then she received the best gift anyone could ever pray for.

Chloe knew that the phone call had come directly from Heaven, and that her new baby was absolutely heaven-sent.

Conclusion

How many times have you called on your loved one who has passed away? No, not telephonically exactly. Your loved one is just a thought away. You can talk to them in your head (telepathically) or even out loud, whatever you feel comfortable with. When my mom passed away I was working in the corporate world, and I set up an e-mail account for her. When things came up that I needed to chat with her about, I would e-mail her. Although I knew she wasn't receiving the e-mails in the way that we receive e-mails, just writing the e-mail was therapeutic, and I was still including her in my life. Every Monday I would give her a list of things I needed help with. It was amazing how there was always resolution, sometimes in the most unexpected ways. It helped me stay present. It helped me stay connected.

Are you calling on your loved ones on the Other Side? Are you picking up on their signals and symbols as they call on you? We all have a direct connection to the Other Side—you simply have to pick up the *phone* to make the call and pick up the *phone* when you hear it ringing. And say *hello*.

Our loved ones are excited and eager to continue to be a part of our lives, and although many have experiences, doubt can creep in. "Do you really think Mom is showing me a sign?" is a question I hear several times a day, just replace *mom* with any other loved one. The answer is, "Yes, yes, I do." We are being provided a continual stream of signs with the hope that you will recognize them.

Be patient, but persistent, in seeking your signs. Always keep an open mind and don't be afraid to ask for a sign. Your loved ones want you to know that you are loved and that they are at peace in the afterlife.

Appendix

When Seeking a Session

A medium reading is a spiritual session where the reader receives information about you in the form of messages, symbols, or images that come from the spiritual plane. A reading is a communication of what your Spirit Guides or loved ones from the Other Side want you to be aware of, and the direction that is best for you at that time.

A good medium reading gives you a new sense of direction. You should be able to relate to parts of the reading, and be able to feel that it is individualized and not just a generic reading. It should confirm what you already know on a conscious level. It should just feel right. Beware of anybody who tells you that you are "cursed" and offers to "break it" for money. They are merely playing on your fears and taking your money!

Here are some handy dos and don'ts to keep in mind when seeking a reading:

DO

- Prepare yourself.
- Have a purpose for your reading.
- Clear your mind.
- Clear your heart.
- Give some feedback—If you feel that the reader is on the wrong track, speak up.
- Take a few deep, cleansing breaths before the reading.
- Try to generate loving, peaceful energy around you.
- Be realistic.
- Take the reading seriously.
- Have a positive attitude.
- Be a good listener.
- Find a reader you have a connection with.
- Have fun!

DON'T

- Don't expect the spiritual counselor to make decisions for you.
- Spiritual counselors can provide good insights, guidance, and second opinions, but they can't—and won't—run your life. Use a reading as an additional source of information.
- Don't think that a reading will fix your life; it should simply guide you. Only you can fix you.
- Don't assume spiritual counselors can predict lottery numbers. The numbers that are chosen are not touched by human hands, thus have no energy within them.

- Don't play games. Playing "Stump the Psychic" is a waste of valuable time and of your own money. It also will make the spiritual counselor lose their enthusiasm and interest in reading for you. Being skeptical is, and should be, welcome, but it is a waste of time to change your name or withhold information.

- Don't have a reading if you have just taken drugs or used alcohol. Even the best readers will have a difficult time seeing through the fog of those substances.

- Don't have a negative attitude. You may just get a reading that focuses on the negativity in your life.

- We all have free will and free choice. What you are told during a session can change depending upon the path you choose and the decisions you make.

- Don't bring children to a reading. A child's energy is strong and erratic and can easily distract even the best reader.

The future is not set in stone and even the best of the best readers can only tell you what is likely to happen, not what *will* happen beyond a shadow of a doubt. We all have free choice and free will, the ability to choose our own thoughts, our own actions, and with whom we spend our time.

Most importantly, a good reading encourages you with hope and inspiration for the future. It also encourages examination of yourself and the direction in which you are headed. You may feel sad after your session, after all it can be very emotional, but you shouldn't feel despondent.

Readings aren't for everyone. I firmly believe that we all have the ability to connect with our loved ones if we just spend time building the connection to the Other Side.

References

Barrett, Sir William. "From Death Bed Visions." Accessed March 2017. http://www.allaboutheaven.org/observations/288/221/mr-durocq-002552.

Dwyer, Jeff. *Ghost Hunters Guide to New Orleans*. Gretna, LA: Pelican Publishing, 2007.

Edwards, Janet Zenke. *Diana of the Dunes: The True Story of Alice Gray*. Charleston, SC: The History Press, 2010.

McKnight, Laura, "May Bailey's Place," April 13, 2015, http://www.nola.com/bar-guide/index.ssf/2015/04/may_baileys_place.html.

Nickell, Joe. *The Mystery Chronicles: More Real-Life X-Files*. Lexington, KT: University of Kentucky, 2004.

Smith, Katherine. *Journey Into Darkness: Ghosts and Vampires of New Orleans*. New Orleans, LA: De Simonin Publications, 1998.

©E. C. Campbell Photography

About the Author

Kristy Robinett is a psychic medium and author who began seeing spirits at the age of three. When she was eight, the spirit of her deceased grandfather helped her escape from a would-be kidnapper, and it was then that Robinett realized the Other Side wasn't so far away. As an adult, she was often called upon by the local police department to examine cold cases in a new light and from a different angle. She gained a solid reputation for being extremely accurate at psychical profiling and giving new perspectives on unsolved crimes. It was then that she began working with a variety of law enforcement agencies, attorneys, and private investigators around the United States, aiding in missing persons, arson, and cold cases. In 2014, she appeared on a one-hour special on the Investigation Network (ID) called *Restless Souls*, spotlighting a police case she assisted on.

Robinett lectures across the country and is a regular media commentator. She is the author of *It's a Wonderful Afterlife*; *Forevermore: Guided in Spirit by Edgar Allan Poe*; *Messenger Between Worlds:*

True Stories from a Psychic Medium; *Higher Intuitions Oracle; Ghosts of Southeast Michigan*; and *Michigan's Haunted Legends and Lore*.

Kristy Robinett is a wife and a mom to four adult children and several animals. She enjoys gardening, cooking, exploring old country towns, porch sitting, and graveyards. In 2016, she and her husband bought their dream farmhouse in rural Michigan.

You can visit her online at KristyRobinett.com, facebook.com /kristyrobinett, or Twitter.com/kristyrobinett.

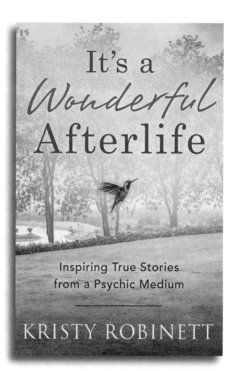

It's a Wonderful Afterlife

Inspiring True Stories
from a Psychic Medium

KRISTY ROBINETT

It's a Wonderful Afterlife
Inspiring True Stories from a Psychic Medium
Kristy Robinett

Reassurance and Hope From the Other Side.

Ever since she was a child, psychic medium Kristy Robinett has communicated with spirits who have shared their experiences of death and what happens afterwards. In this collection of heartwarming stories that answer the most common questions about the afterlife, Robinett delves into the nature of Heaven, if there is a Hell, and what the transition to the Other Side is like. With personal experiences and stories from clients, Kristy explores the many signs and symbols that our loved ones share with us to assure that it is, indeed, a wonderful afterlife.

978-0-7387-4073-7, 240 pp., 5 ¼ x 8   **$15.99**

Messenger Between Worlds
True Stories from a Psychic Medium
KRISTY ROBINETT

Since the age of three, spirits have come to me in the dead of night, telling me of their woes. Kristy Robinett shares the dramatic, touching, and terrifying moments from her extraordinary life as a psychic medium.

This captivating, powerful memoir is filled with unforgettable scenes: spot-on predictions, countless spirit visits at home and school, menacing paranormal activity, rescue from abduction thanks to her loving grandfather in spirit, and Kristy's first meeting with two spirit guides who become her constant allies. Follow her emotional journey though a difficult childhood, stormy marriages, conflict with faith, job loss, and illness—and the hard-won lessons that opened her heart to true love and acceptance of her unique gift.

978-0-7387-3666-2, 288 pp., 5 ¼ x 8   **$14.99**

To order, call 1-877-NEW-WRLD or visit llewellyn.com
Prices subject to change without notice